bake a difference

A compilation of delicious cakes, bakes and savoury recipes made with fair trade ingredients from around the world

Compiled for Traidcraft
by Bee Rawlinson

TRAIDCRAFT
Fighting poverty through trade

Zwena and Shadia trying
local honey.
Photo: Richard Else

contents

First published in Great Britain by Traidcraft plc 2014
Traidcraft plc, Kingsway, Gateshead, NE11 0NE

ISBN: 978-0-9927521-0-1

Designed by GHP Design
Food photography by Bee Rawlinson
and www.shutterstock.com
Cover photograph by Magenta Photographic Studio
Project managed by Carolyn Reynolds
Title by Robot Food
Proofread by Claire Berry
Special thanks to Deb Atkinson, Larry Bush, Jenny File,
Jon McNaughton and Jayne Peebles at Traidcraft

Printed and bound in the UK.

Most of the props used to stage our photography are from
Traidcraft's range of fair trade crafts sourced from around the world.
See more crafts and the full range of
Traidcraft food and baking ingredients at

www.traidcraftshop.co.uk

introduction

When I was first asked to bring together the recipes included in this book, I thought I knew about fair trade food. Which of us hasn't picked up the odd pack of sugar, bar of chocolate or coffee, tea, raisins or nuts in the supermarket and noticed the Fairtrade mark sitting on the corner?

But like most people, I don't think I'd ever realised that for more than thirty years, a whole movement has been working to improve the lives of smallholder farmers across the world through fair trade. The very fact that a pack of sugar sits on the supermarket shelves at all is largely a result of this incredible force for change and a bunch of amazing people.

So imagine the power of that movement when they were asked to produce recipes for this book, a book which encourages the use of the ingredients they've championed for years.

The result? Inspiring recipes, of course. But inspiring stories too. People who really understand the meaning of the word justice, and who are prepared to use their power as consumers to make it happen.

Every single recipe we received was tested, so more than once I heard a knock on the door and experienced the delight of opening a Traidcraft parcel stacked with good things.

Lifting out jars and bottles of golden honey from Chile and Guatemala, plump and juicy raisins from Africa, nuts from India, sugar from Mauritius, dried apricots from Pakistan, dates and almonds from Palestine and chocolate from the Cote D'Ivoire, I felt a connection with communities all over the world as I baked (and baked... and baked...!).

It's been a real pleasure, and one I hope you'll share as you try the recipes in this book.

Enjoy!

Bee

P.S. Because the availability of fair trade is growing all the time, I haven't indicated the fair trade ingredients within the recipes themselves. Please bake a difference and use fair trade whenever you can.

bake a difference

When we first came up with the idea to make a beautiful cookbook featuring wonderful fair trade ingredients, we knew exactly where to go for help.

We put out the word around our fair trade networks up and down the country and asked for favourite recipes so that we could showcase all the delicious things to be done when you bake a difference with fair trade.

We weren't disappointed.

It was clear that the idea of a fair trade cookbook had really taken hold when one of the first recipes to arrive came in the form of a beautifully illustrated leaflet from Bridget Andrews, a Traidcraft supporter. Delicious recipes, to be sure, but also a hymn of praise for the ingredients she'd used to make them. Thanks Bridget!

And the recipes just kept coming.

Each and every one was tested by professional cookery writer Bee Rawlinson before being photographed and considered for the book. It was wonderful to receive so many great recipes, and our thanks to everyone who contributed their favourite.

Choosing the recipes to be included was tough, and it would have been great to have included them all. But as you'd expect with such a big project there were quite a few duplicates, and one or two gaps. So we asked Bee to choose the best and fill in some of the gaps with her own delicious goodies to make for a balanced book. So if the recipe doesn't have a name beneath the title, it's one of Bee's.

Can we ask for your help just one more time? We'd love this book to be a huge success. Because in an increasingly competitive fair trade market where it's harder and harder for small producers to compete, it's one more way to tell the fair trade story, to promote fair trade, and to support smallholder farmers and their families in the developing world.

Thanks. We couldn't do it without you.

All my favourite Fairtrade recipes using 2013 ♥ love these

My Favourite FAIRTRADE ♥ Recipes ♥ using the finest TRAIDCRAFT ingredients.

TRAIDCRAFT really do produce the best Fairtrade food stuffs ♥ keep up your fab work!

savoury Rice

This is the most lovely quality rice and tastes wonderful ☺ It's worth every penny

will take a little longer to cook

10 oz Traidcraft Basmati white rice / brown rice or quinoa

1 pint vegetable stock

½ head celery

1 onion

1 leek

4 oz frozen peas

or try swiss chard, which is very easy to grow in your garden & is similar to spinach

lid, pour oil gently cook, stock with boiling water the quick stir to knock washed spinach Cover

Deena delivering and weighing tea at the Karakorai Small Tea Grower Society Photo: Rajendra Shaw.

charts, weights & conversions

Oven temperatures

Gas Mark	°C	°F	Description
¼	110	225	Very cool
½	120	250	Very cool
1	140	275	Cool
2	150	300	Cool
3	160	325	Warm
4	180	350	Moderate
5	190	375	Moderately hot
6	200	400	Fairly hot
7	220	425	Hot
8	230	450	Very hot
9	240	475	Very hot

Weights

Imperial	Metric
½ oz	15g
1 oz	25g
2oz	50g
3oz	75g
4oz	125g
5oz	150g
6oz	175g
7oz	200g
8oz	225g
9oz	250g
10oz	275g
11oz	300g
12oz	350g
13oz	375g
14oz	400g
15oz	425g
1lb	450g
1lb 2oz	500g
2lb	900g
2¼lb	1kg

Volumes

Imperial	Metric
1fl oz	25ml
2fl oz	50ml
3fl oz	75ml
3½fl oz	100ml
4fl oz	120ml
5fl oz	150ml
6fl oz	175ml
7fl oz	200ml
8fl oz	250ml
10fl oz/ ½ pint	300ml
12fl oz	360ml
14fl oz	400ml
15fl oz	450ml
1 pint	600ml
1¼ pints	750ml
1½ pints	900ml
1¾ pints	1 litre

cakes

Quick and easy, tried and tested, cakes,
traybakes, cupcakes and muffins.
Just stock up your fair trade store
cupboard and bake a difference!

Auntie Glad's Lemon Cake

Recipe donated by Mary Watson Nunziato
*This is my all time favourite recipe, given to me by a church friend.
It's a scrumptious, delicious and refreshing cake.*

Method

1. Preheat oven to 180°C/gas mark 4.

2. Grease and line a swiss roll tin.

3. Grate the lemon rind into a bowl and add the flour. Mix thoroughly.

4. In a separate bowl mix together the lemon juice and caster sugar.

5. Melt the margarine or butter in a heatproof bowl until liquid, then add the demerara sugar and stir until it has dissolved. Add the beaten eggs.

6. Add the liquid ingredients to the flour and lemon zest and mix until you have a smooth batter, then pour into the lined tin. Bake for 20 minutes.

7. Remove from the oven and allow to cool for 5 minutes in the tin before spooning over the lemon juice/caster sugar mixture. Leave to cool completely before cutting into pieces.

Ingredients
Makes approx.12 pieces

2 large eggs, beaten
150g self-raising flour
150g margarine or butter
150g demerara sugar
100g caster sugar
1 large lemon

The people behind the products
Joyce Chibouro, Sugar Cane Farmer

"Because of fair trade we have clean water and electricity. We never believed this would be possible. Tell people that they have made Joyce, a sugar farmer in Malawi, very happy."

Vanilla Cup Cakes

Ingredients
Makes 12

150g self-raising flour
150g caster sugar
150g softened butter
  or margarine
3 large eggs
1 tsp vanilla extract
2 tsp hot water (optional)
decorations

Method

1. Preheat oven to 170°C/gas mark 3.

2. Line a 12 hole muffin tray with muffin cases.

3. Place everything in a large mixing bowl and beat with an electric mixer until combined. The mixture should drop softly from a spoon when tapped on the side of the bowl. If it seems a bit too stiff add hot water a tablespoon at a time until the desired consistency is reached.

4. Divide evenly between the muffin cases. Bake in the centre of the oven for 15-20 minutes or until golden brown and spring back lightly when pressed. Remove to a cooling rack and leave until completely cool.

5. Decorate with fondant icing, fondant flowers, edible glitter, buttercream, sprinkles... the choice is endless!

Tasty tips
For lemon cakes add the grated zest and juice of a lemon and leave out the hot water.
For chocolate cakes replace one tablespoon of flour with one of fair trade cocoa powder.

lots of reasons to love bees

Honey. It's one of our favourite baking ingredients, and one of our favourite ways to help farmers too.

Around 20 years ago, a keen young Traidcraft sourcing staffer named Joe heard about a small group of beekeepers based 12,000 kilometres south of Santiago in the Valdivia province of Chile who wanted to sell fair trade honey.

Joe said 'OK', and after five years of selling their quality honey at fair trade prices, Apicoop became a sustainable co-operative and bought a honey processing plant.

This was great news for local farmers. Without the support of Apicoop, which buys and sells their honey, many families would struggle to make ends meet.

Land is poor here, farming is difficult, and in such a rural area, paid work is scarce. For a family, relying on just one product for almost everything they need can be a risky business.

Apicoop decided to diversify. They wanted to grow and export blueberries. So they bought and cleared 21 hectares of rough ground, ready to cultivate a new crop.

Traidcraft helped Apicoop purchase the first blueberry plants, and our advance payment for their first harvest meant they could buy an essential tool for their blueberry field. A tractor. So next time you're spooning honey into a recipe, remember the Apicoop tractor. A tractor named Joe.

"Believe me, with fair trade, the quality of life for these people has increased. If you are properly paid for what you do then your life changes for the better."

Chino Henriquez, General Manager, Apicoop, Chile

Chino Henriquez and
Juan Inostroza with
the blueberry bushes
in flower
Photo: Richard Else

Rainbow Cake

Method

1. Base line and grease 2 x 18cm loose-bottomed cake tins. Preheat oven to 160°C/gas mark 3.

2. Put all the cake ingredients into a mixing bowl and beat with a wooden spoon or electric mixer until light and fluffy. Split the mixture between two bowls into equal amounts. It's helpful to weigh the empty bowl first, then calculate the total weight of the mixture before dividing in two.

3. Using a cocktail stick or the end of a teaspoon handle add red food colouring to one bowl. Be cautious with the colouring, it is very concentrated so you will only need the equivalent of a drop or so and when baked the colour will be much brighter than the raw batter. Mix the colouring in thoroughly then transfer to one of the tins, spreading out to the edges and levelling the mixture as much as possible. Repeat with the orange food colouring and the mixture in the other bowl.

4. Bake the cakes for 25-30 minutes. Allow to cool in the tin for 5 minutes, then transfer to a cooling rack to finish cooling completely. Re-line the tins and repeat with yellow and green colouring, followed by blue and indigo.

5. Make the buttercream: Melt the white chocolate in a heatproof bowl set over a pan of simmering water, stirring occasionally until liquid. Set aside to cool for about 10 minutes. Beat the butter until soft and fluffy then beat in the icing sugar a third at a time, followed by the milk and then the white chocolate.

6. Assemble the cake: Once the cakes are completely cold place the indigo cake in the centre of a cake board and use a spatula to cover the top with a very thin coating of buttercream. Place the blue layer on top and repeat, followed, in order, by green, yellow, orange and finish with red on the top.

7. Using the spatula cover the whole cake in a thin coating of buttercream. Don't worry too much if a few crumbs are dislodged, this is called a 'crumb coat' – think of it as the undercoat. Place the iced cake in the fridge for 30 minutes to allow the buttercream to set.

8. After 30 minutes apply a second, more generous layer of icing, aim for as smooth a finish as possible. Return to the fridge for at least an hour before serving.

Ingredients

Serves 16

For two cakes (you will need 6 in total):

100g self-raising flour

100g caster sugar

100g butter or margarine

2 eggs

1 tsp vanilla extract food colouring*

White chocolate buttercream:

175g white chocolate, chopped

250g unsalted butter, softened

500g icing sugar

3 tbsp milk

*For this cake you need concentrated food paste colouring. The liquid colours you can buy are not suitable. Food paste colouring is available online or from a cake supply shop.

Rhubarb Crumble Cake

Recipe donated by Sue Hodgman

This cake has a lovely light ginger sponge for the base. If you don't like ginger you can use a teaspoon of vanilla extract instead. It's lovely with a little single cream poured over.

Ingredients

Serves 12

150g self-raising flour

150g butter or soft margarine

150g golden caster sugar

3 large eggs

1 tsp ground ginger

500g rhubarb, cut into 1cm pieces

50g raw cane sugar

100g plain flour

75g butter, melted

75g demerara sugar

Method

1. Preheat oven to 170°C/gas mark 3.

2. Line a 33 x 20cm tin with baking parchment.

3. Use an electric mixer or food processor to mix together the self-raising flour, butter, caster sugar, eggs and ground ginger, then spoon into the tray and level the top with the back of a spoon.

4. Mix together the rhubarb and raw cane sugar and scatter over the sponge batter. This amount should be enough to fit snugly.

5. Use a fork to mix the flour, melted butter and sugar until it clumps together, then sprinkle this mixture over the rhubarb.

6. Bake in the centre of the oven for approximately 40 minutes until the topping is golden and the rhubarb is tender.

7. Allow to cool in the tin, then lift out using the parchment.

8. Cut into 12 squares and serve with single cream.

Honey Apricot Spice Cake

Recipe donated by Sue Ross
This is one of those recipes you keep on a tatty old bit of folded paper in the kitchen drawer – we love it!

Method

1. Preheat oven to 160°C/gas mark 3.
2. Butter a 7 inch square cake tin.
3. Warm the honey over a pan of water.
4. Sift the flour, bicarbonate of soda, ginger, cinnamon and cloves into a mixing bowl.
5. Add the sugar and orange and lemon zest.
6. Rub the butter into the flour until it resembles breadcrumbs.
7. Mix in the egg and honey with 3 tablespoons of water.
8. Beat well, then stir in the apricots.
9. Bake for around 30 minutes and allow to cool in the tin for 5 minutes before turning out onto a cooling rack.
10. To make the icing, sift the icing sugar into a bowl, add lemon juice and water until smooth. Drizzle over the cake.

Ingredients
Makes 9 pieces

75g set honey
250g plain flour
1 tsp ground ginger
1 tsp ground cinnamon
½ tsp ground cloves
75g golden caster sugar
Zest of 1 lemon
Zest of 1 orange
100g butter
1 egg
1 tsp bicarbonate of soda
75g dried apricots, blended to a paste

Icing:
100g icing sugar
tbsp lemon or orange juice
2 tbsp water

St. Clement's Cake

Recipe donated by Beverly Rawlinson

This is a lovely damp cake which is gluten and dairy free. Served just warm with a spoonful of whipped cream it makes a really lovely pudding. You can use another orange in place of the lemon if you prefer.

Ingredients

Serves 6

1 large orange, scrubbed and roughly chopped, include skin but discard any pips

1 large lemon, scrubbed and roughly chopped, include skin but discard any pips

5 eggs, separated

200g ground almonds

200g caster sugar

2 tbsp flaked almonds

Icing sugar to decorate

Gluten and dairy free

Method

1. Preheat oven to 180°C/gas mark 4.

2. Line the base and sides of a 22cm springform baking tin with non-stick baking parchment.

3. Put the chopped fruit in a small saucepan with 1 tablespoon of water and simmer for about 30 minutes or until the fruit is very soft. Allow to cool then purée in a blender or food processor.

4. Whisk the egg whites until they reach the stiff peak stage then add 100g of the caster sugar and whisk for another minute.

5. In another bowl whisk the egg yolks and the remaining 100g of caster sugar until pale and quite thick. Then fold in the fruit purée followed by the ground almonds.

6. Stir in a third of the egg whites to loosen the mixture, then carefully and thoroughly fold in the rest.

7. Transfer the mixture to the prepared tin and smooth the top. Sprinkle with flaked almonds.

8. Bake in the centre of the oven for 50 - 55 minutes or until golden brown and a skewer inserted into the centre of the cake comes out clean. Check the cake after 30 minutes and cover with foil if it appears to be browning too quickly.

9. Leave the cake in the tin and allow to cool completely. Once cool, remove from the tin and carefully peel away the baking parchment. Put onto a plate and dust with icing sugar before serving.

10. It can be kept in an airtight container for up to two days.

Allotment Cake

Recipe donated by Sarah Miller
This is a really easy and delicious cake that uses up all the things that you always seem to have too much of on the allotment!

Method

1. Preheat oven to 170°C/gas mark 3.

2. Grease and flour a 30 x 23cm tin.

3. Mix together the oil and sugar until all the sugar dissolves.

4. Mix in the lightly beaten eggs.

5. Stir in the rhubarb and grated carrots.

6. Add all the dry ingredients and beat to combine. Turn the mixture into the greased and floured cake tin.

7. Bake in the oven for about 60 minutes, until the top is golden brown and a skewer inserted comes out clean. Allow to cool on a wire rack before serving.

Ingredients

Makes 16 pieces

360ml vegetable oil

400g golden caster sugar

2 eggs beaten

300g carrots or courgettes, grated

200g rhubarb stewed with a little sugar until just soft

140g walnuts

275g plain flour

1 tsp baking soda

½ tsp salt

1 tsp ground cinnamon

1 tsp vanilla extract

Tasty tips
A cream cheese icing is nice on this, and it's great with custard too.

Marmalade Cake

Recipe donated by Mary Hollows
We always took this on caravan holidays around the continent when the children were small. It is a lovely cake which stays nice and moist. Mind you, it always gets eaten too fast to have a chance to go stale!

Ingredients
Serves 8

100g self-raising flour
100g ground almonds
100g soft butter
100g brown sugar
2 eggs
4 tbsp fine cut marmalade
juice of one satsuma
pinch of salt

Method

1. Preheat oven to 180°C/gas mark 4.

2. Using the 'all in one method' – put everything in a food processor until combined. Alternatively you can use an electric food mixer and bowl.

3. Place in greased, lined, 450g loaf tin.

4. Cook for 1 hour, but check after 45 minutes as ovens vary.

Top tip
For a shallower cake, use a lined 23cm square tin instead.

Banana Cake

Recipe donated by Joanna Pollard

Method

1. Preheat oven to 170°C/gas mark 3.

2. Line a 1kg loaf tin with baking parchment.

3. In a large mixing bowl cream the butter and sugar together until light and fluffy.

4. Add the eggs one at a time, beating well between adding. The mixture may look a bit curdled, but this is fine.

5. Add the bananas and the dried fruit, mixing in thoroughly.

6. Fold in the flour using a metal spoon.

7. Pour the cake mix into the loaf tin and bake for an hour or until the top is golden and a skewer inserted into the centre of the cake comes out clean.

8. Leave the cake to cool in the tin for 10 minutes before turning out onto a rack to cool completely.

Ingredients

Serves 8

200g self-raising flour

3 large ripe bananas, mashed

150g mixed dried fruit

2 large eggs

125g golden caster sugar

100g butter

Salted Caramel Choc Chip Cookie Bars

Ingredients

Makes 12 pieces

320g plain flour

1 tsp bicarbonate of soda

1 tsp salt

225g butter

150g soft light brown sugar

150g granulated sugar

2 eggs

2 tsp vanilla extract

300g chopped chocolate
(I use a mix of dark, milk
and white fair trade bars)

For the salted caramel:

75g unsalted butter, melted

50g soft light brown sugar

50g caster sugar

50g golden syrup

125ml double cream

Maldon salt or Cornish
sea salt (not table salt!)

Method

1. Preheat oven to 170°C/gas mark 3.

2. Grease a 23cm square baking tin.

3. Make the caramel: melt the butter, sugar and syrup in a small pan and simmer for about 3 minutes, stirring until all is fully melted. Add the cream plus half a teaspoon of salt and stir well. Allow to cool while you make the cookie dough.

4. Sift the flour, bicarbonate of soda and salt into a bowl.

5. In another bowl, using an electric mixer, cream together the butter, both sugars and vanilla extract until light and fluffy.

6. Add the eggs one at a time, beating well after each is added.

7. Gradually add the flour and then stir in the chopped chocolate.

8. Spoon half the cookie dough into the tin and level with the back of a metal spoon. I find dipping the spoon in some cold water makes this easier. Spoon an even layer of caramel over the dough - aim for around half a centimetre - then carefully dot the top with spoonfuls of the remaining dough and gently blend together with the back of the spoon until all the caramel is covered.

9. Bake for 30 minutes or until the top is a light golden brown and the edges are beginning to pull away from the tin. Cool on a rack in the tin then cover and transfer to the fridge for 30 minutes before cutting into squares. Store in an airtight container at room temperature.

Butter Tarts

Method

1. Preheat oven to 190°C/gas mark 5.

2. Mix the sugar, butter and beaten eggs together. Stir in the vinegar, then add the mixed fruit and nuts.

3. Line patty tins with pastry and put a spoonful of the mixture into each.

4. Bake on the middle shelf of the oven for 25-30 minutes. Eat warm or cold.

Ingredients
Makes 12

2 eggs, beaten

50g chopped walnuts

250g shortcrust pastry

200g soft brown sugar

1 tbsp vinegar

250g mixed dried fruit

125g butter, melted

bake a difference

Currently less than 2% of sugar sold worldwide is fair trade. Please use fair trade sugar in your baking.

Date & Walnut Scones

Recipe donated by Helen Falconer-Flint

I made these fluffy scones with what I had in the cupboard one day when I'd run out of mixed fruit. Now they're firm family fair trade favourites!

Ingredients

Makes 8

225g self-raising flour
pinch of salt
50g butter
25g golden caster sugar
50g dates finely chopped
25g walnuts
1 egg
milk to make up to 5fl oz
 with egg

Method

1. Preheat oven to 200°C/gas mark 6.

2. Sift the flour and salt together. Rub in the butter and stir in the sugar. Stir in the dates and walnuts.

3. Beat the egg and milk together, add to the mixture using a knife to bring together.

4. Pull together with hands to a rolling out consistency but don't overwork.

5. Roll out to around 1cm thick. Cut into 8 rounds.

6. Bake for 15-18 minutes and cool on a rack.

bake a difference

"Your dates are so delicious they rarely get into my baking without me opening a second packet."

more than just chocolate

A four hour 'african massage'. That's the treat on offer when we visit some of our more remote cocoa producers in Cote D'Ivoire, where the ridged and potholed dirt tracks provide some bumpy therapy.

For Traidcraft, the more remote, the better. Unlike bigger chocolate companies, we actively choose groups that are most vulnerable, poor or remote – in short, the hardest to trade with. That's because they're the farmers and communities who can most benefit from our help.

The co-operatives we work with on cocoa in the Cote D'Ivoire are a good example of the way we work with hundreds of smallholder farmers, co-operatives and groups of growers across the developing world.

We start with the simple things, and for cocoa, that means proper pruning. Farmers often prune and fertilise cocoa plants exactly the way their fathers and grandfathers did, planting trees too close together. That means poorer air circulation, more disease, poorer crops and harder work. Simple training to chop off the right branches at the right time of year can mean a third more cocoa at no extra cost to the farmer.

When it comes to getting a fair price and the bonus of Fairtrade premium money to spend in the community, it's the simple things that are important for farmers, their families and their communities too.

A borehole that provides fresh, clean water for the whole village. An education for their children. A bridge to get cocoa from the fields in the rainy season. Even, in time, a tractor.

Buy fair trade and you support farmers, families and communities to trade their own way out of poverty. It's that simple.

Celebration Chocolate Cake

Recipe donated by Susan Faragher

This rich but light cake makes a great treat for a special occasion. It's adding the meringue that makes the difference. I've made it with a lovely white chocolate buttercream filling but it's also great with chocolate icing and dark chocolate curls – freezes beautifully too.

Ingredients

200g butter
300g caster sugar
  for cake
50g sugar for meringue
6 free range local eggs,
  separated
300g dark chocolate,
  melted
300g self-raising flour

White chocolate icing:
100g white chocolate
200g icing sugar
little knob of butter
2 tbsp milk or cream

**Chocolate
mascarpone icing:**
200g mascarpone
2 tbsp cocoa powder
100g icing sugar
2 tbsp of milk

Method

1. Preheat oven to 180°C/gas mark 4.

2. Grease and base line a 25cm square tin.

3. In a large mixing bowl cream the butter and sugar together, then whisk in the egg yolks. Stir in the melted chocolate.

4. Whisk egg whites until stiff, then add the extra 50g sugar and continue whisking until you have a glossy meringue mixture.

5. Sift in the flour and fold it and the meringue into the chocolate mix with a large metal spoon.

6. Transfer the mix to the greased square cake tin and bake for 45-55 minutes, or until a skewer inserted into the centre of the cake comes out clean. Leave to cool in the tin for 10 minutes then remove and allow to cool completely on a cake rack.

7. For white chocolate icing: Melt white chocolate and butter over hot water, sift in the icing sugar and the milk beating until smooth. If the icing is too stiff add a tablespoon of hot water.

8. For the chocolate mascarpone icing: Beat all the ingredients together until you have a smooth icing.

9. Use a long serrated knife to split the cake in half horizontally, a bread knife is ideal for this. Spread the white chocolate icing evenly on the bottom layer and replace the top. Spread the top of the cake with chocolate mascarpone icing. Decorate with sifted cocoa powder, chocolate curls etc.

Jaffa Cup Cakes

Method

1. Preheat oven 170°C/gas mark 3.

2. Line a 12 hole muffin tin with cup cake cases.

3. Put the first seven ingredients into a mixing bowl and beat until smooth. Divide equally between the cup cake cases.

4. Bake on the middle shelf for 15-20 minutes until risen and golden. Allow to cool in the tin for 10 minutes then remove from the tin and cool completely on a rack.

5. Scoop out a teaspoonful of cake from the middle of each one and fill with a teaspoon of marmalade.

6. Cover each cake with a spoonful of melted chocolate and allow to cool and set.

Ingredients

Makes 12

100g self-raising flour

100g soft butter or margarine

100g golden caster sugar

50g ground almonds

2 eggs

½ tsp almond extract

Grated rind of 1 orange

12 tsp orange marmalade

100g dark chocolate, melted

bake a difference

A 1% increase in their share of world trade would generate five times what Africa receives in aid.

Chocolate & Beetroot Cake

Recipe donated by Bridget Andrews

This is a moist and delicious cake, full of fair trade goodness. You could change the beetroot for stem ginger from a jar for a change – add a few pieces, chopped.

Ingredients

Makes 12 slices

150g dark chocolate, chopped

150g butter

150g golden caster sugar

3 eggs, separated

50g ground almonds

120g self-raising flour

1 tbsp cocoa powder

250g cooked beetroot

Method

1. Preheat oven to 190°C/gas mark 5.

2. Grease and line a large loaf tin.

3. Melt the chocolate gently over a pan of simmering water then remove from the heat and cool.

4. Beat butter and sugar until light and fluffy then add the egg yolks one at a time, making sure to beat well after each addition.

5. Beat in the cooled chocolate.

6. Sift in ground almonds, flour and cocoa and fold in.

7. Purée or mash beetroot and fold in gently using a large metal spoon.

8. In a clean bowl with clean beaters, whisk egg whites until stiff peaks form, then fold in the chocolate and beetroot mixture.

9. Spoon into the prepared tin and bake for 40 minutes or until skewer inserted in the centre of the cake comes out clean.

10. Remove from the oven and allow to cool in the tin for 5 minutes, then transfer carefully to a cooling rack.

bake a difference

Just over 1% of all the cocoa grown in the world is sold as fair trade. Using fair trade chocolate really matters.

Lemon & Lavender Cake

Method

1. Preheat oven 160°C/gas mark 3.

2. Grease and line 2 x 20cm loose bottomed cake tins.

3. Put the flour, butter, sugar, eggs, lemon zest and juice into a food processor and whizz until combined. Divide the mixture evenly between the two tins and level with the back of a spoon. Bake in the preheated oven for 25-30 minutes until the tops are golden and spring back when lightly pressed. Allow to cool in the tins.

4. Put the mascarpone and icing sugar in a bowl and beat together until smooth. Stir in the lavender.

5. Sandwich the cakes together with the lemon curd and half the mascarpone cream. Spread the remaining mascarpone over the top of the cake and decorate with lavender flowers.

Ingredients

Serves 8

150g self-raising flour
150g butter or margarine
150g golden caster sugar
3 eggs
zest and juice of a lemon
1 tsp dried lavender
200g mascarpone
100g icing sugar
100g lemon curd

Optional: Lavender flowers for decoration

Tasty tips

Lavender goes very well with lemon but if it doesn't appeal you can substitute 1 teaspoon fresh lemon thyme leaves.

Chocolate Squares

Recipe donated by Jill Cliff
This is my favourite fair trade recipe, easy to make and very scrummy. It was one of the recipes I used to make when I first left university in 1992 and I still love making it now.

Ingredients

Makes roughly 20 squares

100g rolled oats

75g coconut

150g soft margarine
  or butter

100g sugar

100g flour

1 tsp cocoa powder

½ tsp baking powder

Icing:

200g icing sugar

2 tsp cocoa powder

3 tsp hot water

Method

1. Preheat oven to 190°C/gas mark 5.

2. Grease a 23cm square tin.

3. Cream together the sugar and margarine or butter.

4. Add all dry ingredients and mix well. Press into the greased tin and bake for 20 minutes.

5. Beat together the icing sugar, cocoa powder and hot water to make a glossy icing. Pour over the base while still hot.

6. When the cake is completely cool, cut into 5cm squares.

Bake a difference

"Fair trade certification for our cocoa was not easy, but it is worth it. Now we have fair contracts and a fair price, a future."

All In Breakfast Muffins

Recipe donated by Helen Falconer-Flint

This is what I laughingly call the healthy option! The apricots give the muffins a lovely tangy flavour.

Ingredients

Makes 12

100g dried apricots
4 tbsp orange juice
2 large eggs
140ml soured cream
100ml sunflower oil
85g caster sugar
300g self-raising flour
1 tsp baking powder
50g muesli
12 tsp marmalade

Topping:
50g light muscovado sugar
2 tbsp sunflower oil
50g muesli

Method

1. Preheat oven 190°C/gas mark 5.

2. Line a 12 hole muffin tin with muffin cases.

3. Soak the apricots in the orange juice for 2-3 hours to soften and plump up.

4. Beat the eggs in a medium bowl, then mix in the soured cream, oil and sugar. Stir in the apricots.

5. Put the flour, baking powder and muesli in a large bowl, then gently stir in the apricot mixture, combining thoroughly but quickly. Don't over-mix.

6. Spoon the mixture into the muffin cases. Make an indent in the top of each muffin and fill with one teaspoon of marmalade.

7. Combine topping ingredients and sprinkle over the top of each muffin.

8. Bake for 25-30 minutes until golden brown.

Helen, Traidcraft's resident baker

Always on hand to run up a batch of perfectly iced cupcakes for birthdays, she also runs a baking 'tuck shop' in the Customer Services Department every Monday. The proceeds support the education of a child in India and a range of local charities.

Honey Cake

Recipe donated by Helen Falconer-Flint
One of those recipes you keep for ages and use again and again.

Method

1. Preheat oven to 160°C/gas mark 3.

2. Butter and line a 20cm round, loose-bottom cake tin.

3. Cut the butter into pieces and put into a non-stick pan along with the honey and sugar. Melt slowly over a low heat. When liquid increase the heat and boil for one minute. Leave to cool.

4. Beat the eggs into the cooled mixture using a wooden spoon. Sift the flour into a large bowl, then pour in the egg and honey mixture, beating until smooth.

5. Pour the batter into the prepared tin and bake for 50-60 minutes until well risen and golden. Turn the cake out onto a wire rack.

6. Warm the 2 tablespoons of honey in a small pan and brush over the top of the cake to glaze. Leave to cool.

Ingredients

Serves 12

225g butter or margarine

250g runny honey, plus 2 tbsp for glaze

100g dark muscovado sugar

3 large eggs, beaten

300g self-raising flour

Cherry & White Chocolate Loaf

Method

1. Preheat the oven to 170°C/gas mark 3.

2. Grease and line a 1kg loaf tin with baking parchment.

3. Cut the cherries into quarters, rinse and blot thoroughly on kitchen paper, dusting them lightly with a little flour.

4. Mix together the flour, baking powder and salt in a bowl.

5. Put the yoghurt, sugar, eggs, almond extract and oil in another bowl and whisk to combine.

6. Fold the dry ingredients quickly but thoroughly into the wet mixture then fold in the cherries and chocolate. Pour the mixture into the lined tin and level the top.

7. Stand the tin on a baking tray and bake for 55-60 minutes or until the top is golden brown and a skewer inserted into the middle of the cake comes out clean. Check after 40 minutes and if the top is browning too quickly cover lightly with foil.

Ingredients

Makes 1 loaf

I used frozen, pitted cherries but fresh or frozen raspberries would make a good substitute.

250g frozen cherries, defrosted

150g plain flour

2 tsp baking powder

½ tsp salt

240ml plain yoghurt

200g raw cane sugar

3 eggs

1 tsp almond extract *

120ml vegetable oil

100g white chocolate, chopped

*If using raspberries add 2 tsp grated lemon zest and ½ tsp vanilla extract instead

Wellington Square (Caramel Shortbread)

Ingredients

Serves 16

Shortbread:
150g caster sugar
300g unsalted butter at room temperature
450g plain flour

Caramel:
100g unsalted butter
100g golden syrup
100g muscovado sugar
1 can of condensed milk

Chocolate Topping:
200g fair trade milk chocolate

Recipe donated by Rachel Whittington

I am just a month younger than Traidcraft. My mum was a Fair Trader from the early 80s till 2011 when I took over her account. Fair trade has always been a part of my life. This is my favourite recipe, I cannot stop baking it. Inheriting my Grandma's mixer has made it easier!

Method

1. Preheat the oven to 180°C/gas mark 4.

To make the shortbread:

2. Cream the butter and sugar.

3. Sift flour and add to creamed butter and sugar.

4. Press into a large Swiss roll tin (I find it's easier to do this with the palms of my hands).

5. Bake for 20-25 minutes. Allow to cool.

To make the caramel:

6. Place all the ingredients in a pan and gently heat to boiling. Boil for 7 minutes.

7. Pour onto the base and allow to cool.

To make the topping:

8. Melt chocolate and spread evenly over the caramel. Allow to cool.

9. Cut into squares.

Tasty tip
Turn the traybake upside down to cut into squares and the chocolate shouldn't crack.

Fruit Slices

Recipe donated by Mags Vaughan
*My friends and family will tell you I'm no sort of baker,
but even I can manage this delicious fruit slice!*

Method

1. Preheat oven 180°C/gas mark 4.

2. Grease a 33 x 20cm tray.

3. Make the pastry. Rub the fat into the flour and salt until it resembles breadcrumbs. Gradually mix in the cold water a tablespoon at a time until a dough forms.

4. Gather together and knead briefly on a floured surface before covering in clingfilm and chilling in the fridge for 30 minutes. Then roll out the pastry and line the greased tray. Prick the base all over with a fork and bake blind for 10 minutes.

5. Cream the butter and sugar together until light and fluffy then add the egg, followed by the ground rice and almonds.

6. Stir in the fruit and nuts. Spread evenly onto the cooked pastry case and sprinkle the top with demerara sugar.

7. Bake for 30-35 minutes until the top is golden.

8. Cool in the tin and cut into slices before serving.

Ingredients
Serves 8-10

100g butter
100g caster sugar
50g ground rice
25g ground almonds
1 egg
100g sultanas
50g walnuts
50g glace or sour cherries
2tbs demerara sugar

Pastry base:
170g plain flour
45g butter
45g lard
pinch of salt
cold water

Auntie Susan's Favourite Apple Cake

Recipe donated by Marylin Smith

This recipe was handed down from my aunt's mother-in-law, who came from Denmark. It is a firm favourite in our house, traditionally eaten at Christmas and Easter by candlelight.

Method

1. Preheat oven 170°C/gas mark 3.

2. Grease and base line a 22cm round springform tin.

3. Cream together the 80g butter and the light brown sugar until light and fluffy. Add in the beaten egg, blend, then mix in the baking soda, salt, cinnamon and nutmeg and beat until well combined.

4. Add the flour and stir thoroughly then add the apples and nut mixture and mix until combined.

5. Spoon the mixture into the cake tin and bake for 30-40 minutes until golden and the top springs back when touched.

6. To make the hot toffee sauce melt the butter in a saucepan then add the sugar and salt. Let it boil then take off the heat and whisk in the vanilla extract and evaporated milk or cream.

7. To serve, slice the cake, place on a plate and spoon warm sauce over the top.

Ingredients

Makes 8-10 pieces

100g chopped mixed fair trade nuts and fruit (e.g. walnuts and sultanas)

450g finely-chopped Granny Smith apples

80g soft butter

150g light brown sugar

1 egg, lightly beaten

1 tsp baking soda

¼ tsp salt

1 tsp cinnamon

½ tsp nutmeg

½ tsp vanilla extract

180g plain flour

For the caramel sauce:

100g butter

150g muscavado sugar

½ tsp salt

1 tsp vanilla extract

120ml cream or evaporated milk

Tiramisu Cake

Recipe donated by Carolyn Reynolds

This is loosely based on the popular Italian pudding Tiramisu, and tastes even better with a cup of freshly brewed fair trade coffee.

Ingredients

Serves 8-10

100g dark muscovado sugar

50g cocoa powder

2 tbsp instant coffee

250ml boiling water

125g butter or margarine

150g golden caster sugar

225g plain flour mixed with 1 tsp baking powder

2 eggs

250g mascarpone cheese

50g icing sugar

50ml Marsala wine

2 tbsp strong coffee

Icing sugar

Method

1. Preheat oven to 180°C/gas mark 4.

2. Line and grease 2 x 20cm loose-bottomed cake tins.

3. Put the sugar, cocoa and coffee in a jug or bowl, add the boiling water and whisk until combined. Allow to cool.

4. Put the butter and caster sugar in a mixing bowl and beat until pale and fluffy. Then add one egg and one tablespoon of flour and continue beating until incorporated.

5. Repeat with the other egg and another tablespoon of the flour, then add the remaining flour.

6. Gradually mix in the cocoa and coffee mixture until you have a smooth runny batter.

7. Divide equally between the cake tins and bake for 30 minutes. Allow to cool in the tins for 5 minutes then transfer to a wire rack and leave to cool completely.

8. Beat together the mascarpone, Marsala and icing sugar and use to sandwich the cakes together.

9. Put the coffee in a bowl and add enough icing sugar to make a thick, runny icing. Pour over the middle of the top cake and allow to spread across the top (some may drip down the sides). Leave to set before cutting.

Apricot Brownies

Recipe donated by Sue Lawrence

Ingredients

Makes 12

350g dark chocolate

250g unsalted butter

250g dark muscovado sugar

1 tsp baking powder

pinch of salt

150g chopped dried apricots

Method

1. Preheat the oven to 170°C/gas mark 3-4.

2. Melt the chocolate and butter together, stir and cool slightly.

3. Whisk the eggs well, beat in the sugar until thick and glossy.

4. Gently fold in the melted chocolate mixture, then sift in the flour and baking powder with a pinch of salt.

5. Pour two-thirds into a buttered 23cm square cake tin, scatter over the apricots, tip over remaining batter and bake for about 35-40 minutes.

6. Test by inserting a wooden cocktail stick into the middle. There should be few moist crumbs adhering. Remove and cool the tin on a wire rack.

7. After about 30 minutes cut into squares and remove to a wire rack to finish cooling.

Welsh Cakes

Recipe donated by Manuela Williams
They seem to taste better if you use the fluted side of a biscuit cutter – strange but true!

Method

1. Rub the butter and lard into the flour until it resembles breadcrumbs, then stir in the sultanas and salt.

2. Mix in the beaten egg and 1 tablespoon of milk and bring the mix together to form a stiff dough. It should feel similar to shortcrust pastry. Add a little more milk if it's too stiff. Roll out to about the thickness of a pound coin, then stamp out rounds with a biscuit cutter.

3. Grease a flat griddle or large frying pan with a little lard and cook for approximately 3 minutes each side until golden brown.

4. Sprinkle with extra granulated sugar and eat warm with a little butter.

Ingredients

Makes 12-14

225g self-raising flour
50g butter
50g lard
75g sultanas
100g granulated sugar
1 egg, beaten
milk
¼ tsp salt

Chantry Chocolate Cake

Recipe donated by the Dumfries Fairtrade Group

This is one of the recipes we posted on our website for Fairtrade Fortnight.

Ingredients

Serves 10-12

100g butter or
margarine

250g caster sugar

2 eggs

50g cocoa powder

230ml water

150g plain flour

¼ tsp salt

1 tsp bicarbonate
of soda

¼ tsp baking powder

Method

1. Preheat oven 180°C/gas mark 4. Line and grease a deep 23cm cake tin.

2. In a mixing bowl beat margarine and sugar together until pale and fluffy. Add eggs one at a time.

3. Mix the cocoa and water together and add to the mixture followed by the all the dry ingredients. Place in the greased and lined tin and bake for 50-60 minutes.

4. Leave to cool in the tin.

5. To make the fudge icing: melt 50g margarine. Add 1 tablespoon of milk, 1 tablespoon of cocoa and beat in enough icing sugar to make a thick smooth icing. Pipe or spread over the cooled cake and allow to set.

bake a difference

Women work two thirds of the world's working hours and produce half the world's food, but earn only 10% of the world's income and make up 70% of the world's poor.

White Chocolate & Walnut Blondies

Method

1. Preheat an oven to 190°C/gas mark 5.

2. Grease and line a 20cm square tin.

3. Break 100g of chocolate into pieces and put in a heatproof bowl along with the butter. Set over a pan of simmering water and leave to melt. Chop the remaining chocolate into small pieces.

4. Beat together the sugar, eggs and vanilla then beat in the melted chocolate mixture.

5. Add the flour, walnuts and chopped chocolate and stir to mix.

6. Put into the prepared tin and spread evenly.

7. Bake for approximately 25 minutes until golden brown and the centre is just firm. Leave to cool in the tin before removing and cut into squares before serving.

Ingredients

Makes 9 pieces

40g butter
200g white chocolate
60g golden caster sugar
1 tsp vanilla extract
2 eggs
75g self-raising flour
50g walnuts, chopped

bake a difference

"I joined the Fair trade co-operative because they trade without cheating. They care about farmers. Now the price for my honey is fair."

Matrimonial Cake

Recipe donated by Dumfries Fairtrade Group
...because you have to take the rough with the smooth!

Ingredients

Serves 9

250g stoned dates

25g muscovado sugar
(for cooking dates)

100ml water

100g porridge oats

75g wholewheat flour

50g muscovado sugar

75g butter or margarine

Method

1. Preheat oven 180°C/gas mark 4.

2. Grease an 18cm square tin.

3. Chop the dates and cook gently with the sugar and water until like a paste, soft but not sloppy. Leave to cool.

4. Mix oats, flour and sugar. Rub in butter until like a crumble mixture.

5. Put half of this mixture into the greased tin and pat down firmly. Spread with the date paste. Cover with the rest of crumble mixture and pat down gently.

6. Bake just above the middle of the oven for 15-20 minutes until golden brown. Cut into squares while still hot then leave to cool in the tin. Lift slices out when cool.

"Like slavery and apartheid, poverty is not a natural state."
Nelson Mandela

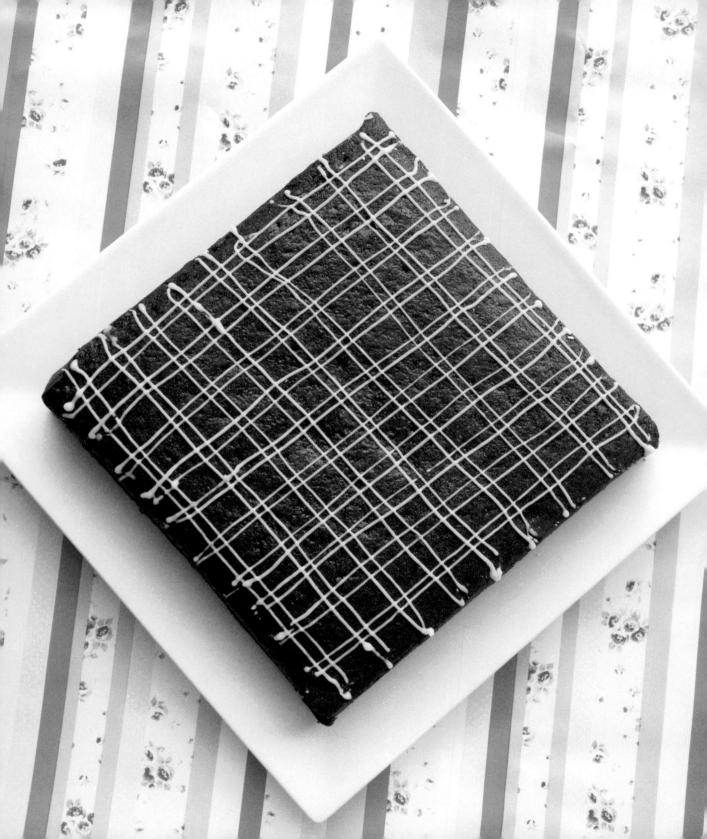

Sticky Gingerbread

Method

1. Preheat the oven to 140°C/gas mark 1.

2. Grease and line a 20cm square tin.

3. Warm the margarine or butter, treacle and syrup together until melted. Whisk in the milk and allow to cool.

4. Sift all the dry ingredients into a mixing bowl. Whisk the eggs into the treacle mixture then add to the bowl. Beat well. Pour into the lined tin.

5. Bake for 1¼ -1½ hours or until a skewer inserted near the centre comes out clean.

6. Allow to cool in the tin for 5 minutes, then transfer out of the tin and onto a cooling rack.

7. When completely cool, mix enough icing sugar with the lemon juice to make a runny icing and use to decorate the cake.

Ingredients
Makes 9 pieces

110g margarine
  or butter
150g black treacle
85g golden syrup
150ml milk
225g plain flour
55g dark muscovado
  sugar
2 eggs
1 tsp mixed spice
1 tsp bicarbonate
  of soda
4 tsp ground ginger
1 tbsp lemon juice
icing sugar

The people behind the products
Joseph Anduthazhyth,
Fair Trade Alliance Kerula

"Depending on the open market is always a problem for farmers. Fair trade gives us a fair return for our coffee."

Peanut Butter Squares

Recipe donated by Helen Falconer-Flint
I cobbled this recipe together from two others. Yummy!

Ingredients

Serves 16

150g butter

200g dark chocolate
or half dark, half milk

250g digestive biscuits

200g soft brown sugar

300g crunchy peanut
butter

1 tsp vanilla extract

Method

1. Line a 23cm square tin with baking parchment (overhang the ends).

2. Melt the butter in a large pan over a low heat.

3. Melt the chocolate in a heatproof bowl over a pan of simmering water, or in the microwave.

4. Blitz the biscuits and brown sugar in a food processor or blender until fine crumbs, then tip them into the melted butter. Add the vanilla extract and peanut butter and stir until well combined.

5. Tip the mixture into the lined tin and press down well.

6. Pour over the melted chocolate and tilt the tin back and forth to ensure the chocolate has covered evenly.

7. Freeze for 30 minutes.

8. Lift out of the tin using the overhanging baking parchment, cut into squares with a sharp knife.

more than just coffee

Sweating in a bee suit high on the side of a Guatemalan volcano, one of our sourcing managers noticed something interesting.

Coffee beans. High grown, high quality, Arabica coffee beans.

Right where they eke out their small earnings from selling their honey, beekeepers were also growing coffee as a cash crop. But because of their remote location, they were forced to sell their coffee to local traders for a very poor price.

These farmers were some of the poorest and most vulnerable we'd ever traded with, farmers who would never trouble the balance sheets of bigger coffee suppliers. Their location is too remote, their land inaccessible, their infrastructure non-existent.

But at Traidcraft we were interested, because we knew that here, fair trade could make a real difference to a whole community. The discovery of these high quality coffee beans was just the start of a very special harvest for the farmers of the CIPAC co-operative.

Over the next three years, we worked with farmers to gain Fairtrade certification for their coffee, and with partners on the other side of the volcano to process the beans, so that more of the value of the crop stayed where it was needed. We developed a supply chain to sell the coffee to customers in the UK.

Now, farmers like Guillermo and Olimipa Perez are seeing the benefits of fair trade. Newly planted fruit trees to help plant pollination and provide fruit for their children, improvements like a new collection centre to help them farm more effectively, and all the training and technical help they need for their coffee and honey.

"The price from Traidcraft is fair, and we get the help we need. I think it is beautiful, because here the local prices vary. In the future we want to grow more coffee so that my children can go to high school, maybe become teachers." Guillermo Perez.

Guillermo and Olimpia
harvesting coffee beans
Photo: Richard Else

loaves

Tea breads, tearing breads and
tasty loaves to try.

Foccacia with Rosemary Sea Salt

Method

1. In a large bowl, combine the yeast and flour; stir well to combine. Stir in ¾ of the water and mix with your hands until a very soft, wet dough comes together (add the rest of the water if needed). Turn out onto a lightly-floured surface and knead briefly for about 2 minutes.

2. Oil a large bowl, place the dough in the bowl and turn to coat with oil. Cover with a damp cloth or clingfilm and let it rise in a warm place until doubled in volume (approximately 30 minutes).

3. Turn the dough out onto a lightly-floured surface and knead briefly, it will deflate quite quickly. Transfer the dough onto a 30cm x 15cm baking sheet or shallow baking tin then gradually push and stretch the dough into the corners until it is an even thickness. Cover with clingfilm and leave in a warm place until it has doubled in thickness.

4. Heat the oven to 230°C/gas mark 9.

5. Remove the clingfilm and using the tips of your fingers poke the dough all over, making deep indentations across the surface. Drizzle with 2 tablespoons of olive oil and sprinkle with chopped rosemary and sea salt.

6. Bake for 15-20 minutes until golden brown. Extra olive oil can be drizzled over before serving if liked.

7. Best served warm.

Ingredients
Serves 6

1 tsp caster sugar

2 sachets quick acting yeast

400ml warm water (this dough should be quite wet, you may need all the water)

500g strong bread flour

2 tbsp olive oil

2 tsp chopped fresh rosemary

½ tsp sea salt crystals

Seedy Treasure Loaf

Recipe donated by Mary Cundy

This loaf is a bit different, but delicious! Tastes good buttered and spread with honey or eaten with cheese or vegetable soup.

Ingredients

Makes 1 loaf

Serves 6

50g wheat germ

50g rice flakes

50g walnuts

25g sunflower seeds

25g pumpkin seeds

25g sesame seeds

25g linseeds

125g maftoul (cous cous)

½ tsp bicarbonate soda

pinch of salt

1 small egg

1 tbsp honey

250ml natural yoghurt
(not fat free)

Method

1. Preheat oven to 180°C/gas mark 4.

2. Line a small loaf tin with baking parchment.

3. Beat together egg, honey and yoghurt. Mix in the dry ingredients and leave to soak for 20 minutes.

4. Pour into tin and bake in oven.

5. After 30 minutes check if cooked by inserting a warmed skewer. If this comes out clean the loaf is cooked. If sticky, cover the tin loosely with foil and cook for a further 10 minutes before checking again.

6. Turn out onto a wire rack to cool.

Fruity Loaf

We're not sure who sent this recipe as it arrived by post with no name, but it is so delicious we had to include it. *Even better after a couple of days in a cake tin.*

Method

1. Preheat oven 160°C/gas mark 3.

2. Grease a 1kg loaf tin.

3. Roughly chop dates and put into a large saucepan with water. Bring to the boil then simmer gently until soft.

4. Remove from heat and mash to a paste with a wooden spoon. Add dried fruit, flour and all other ingredients.

5. Spoon into your chosen tin and sprinkle the top with almonds, if using.

6. Bake for 90 minutes.

7. This can be made with other flours such as gluten free or spelt, and other dried fruits of choice.

Ingredients

Makes 1 loaf

200g dates
280ml water
3 tsp baking powder
500g mixed fruit
1 tsp mixed spice
170g plain whole
  wheat flour
4 tbsp orange juice
50g ground almonds
Grated rind of an
  orange or lemon
Flaked almonds for
  topping (optional)

Egg free
and
fat free!

Easy Pleasy Bara Brith

Recipe donated by Anne Gee

This is a great favourite of the family and so easy to do – the chopped apricots give it an enhanced flavour. I share this with my friends, the 'lightship ladies' – we met when we used to work as volunteers at The Lightship, a Christian centre in Cardiff Bay. The friendship and fellowship we share is still as strong as ever. Coffee, cake and a good chat – what's not to like?

Ingredients

Makes 1 loaf

50g dried apricots, chopped

150g raisins

150g sultanas
  (or 350g dried mixed fruit)

140g dark muscovado sugar

300ml strong hot tea

275g self-raising flour

½ tsp mixed spice

1 large free range egg,
  beaten

Method

1. Preheat oven to 130°C/gas mark ½.

2. Put the dried fruit and sugar into a large bowl.

3. Pour over the hot tea and leave to soak overnight or at least 2-3 hours to allow the fruit to swell up.

4. Add the sifted flour and spice and the beaten egg and give a very good stir to mix thoroughly.

5. Put into a lined or greased 2lb/900g loaf tin and bake in preheated oven for 1½ hours. Loaf should be well risen. A skewer inserted into the middle should come out clean.

6. Put the tin on a wire rack and leave loaf in the tin for about 10 minutes before turning out.

Tasty tips

Delicious served warm. Slice and spread with a little bit of butter and a nice cup of freshly brewed fair trade tea. Enjoy!

puddings

Naughty but nice desserts with the sweet taste of justice in every bite. Go on. Bake the difference with a fair trade pud!

Border Tart

Recipe donated by Sylvia Harris
I've been a Traidcraft supporter for 22 years, since I moved to the Borders. This recipe was one of the first I was given when I came to live in Northumberland and I've made it ever since.

Method

1. Preheat oven to 190°C/gas mark 5.

2. To make the pastry, rub the flour and butter together, add the ground almonds, caster sugar and egg yolk with 1 tablespoon of cold water. Chill for 30 minutes.

3. Roll out the pastry and use it to line a 23cm (9in) loose-bottomed, fluted tart tin. Prick the bottom with a fork and chill for a further 30 minutes.

4. Line the pastry case with greaseproof paper. Fill with baking beans and bake for 15 minutes, then remove the paper and beans and cook for a further 10-15 minutes till just baked. Leave to cool.

5. For the filling, beat together the butter and sugar, then stir in the eggs, raisins, sultanas and cinnamon with the grated rind of one orange.

6. Tip into the pastry case and bake for 30 minutes until set. (You might need to cover it loosely with foil for the last 10 minutes or so to prevent the raisins burning.)

7. Allow to cool in the tin for a while, then put on wire rack.

8. Mix the sifted icing sugar with about 3 tablespoons of water to make a smooth icing. Drizzle over the tart and sprinkle with the remaining grated orange rind. Delicious served warm with cream or ice cream.

Ingredients

For the pastry:
175g plain flour
125g unsalted butter
25g ground almonds
25g caster sugar
1 egg yolk

For the filling:
100g unsalted butter, softened
100g dark muscovado sugar
2 large eggs, beaten
200g raisins
200g sultanas
2 small oranges, rind finely grated
½ tsp ground cinnamon
125g icing sugar, sifted, plus extra to dust

Coffee Cream Torte

Ingredients

Serves approx 10

450g butter

170ml strong black coffee

450g dark chocolate, broken into pieces

200g cane sugar

50ml Irish liqueur (optional)

6 eggs

Method

1. Preheat oven to 160°C/gas mark 3.

2. Grease a 20cm springform tin and base line it with baking parchment.

3. In a large pan melt the butter, coffee, liqueur (if using) and sugar over a low heat until the sugar has dissolved.

4. Add the chocolate pieces and stir until melted and the mixture is smooth and glossy. Remove from the heat.

5. Using an electric mixer whisk the eggs until they are pale yellow and have tripled in volume.

6. Stir a third of the whisked eggs into the chocolate mixture to loosen it, then fold in the rest.

7. Pour the batter into the lined tin and bake for 50-60 minutes. It is ready when the sides are starting to puff and crack but the centre is still a bit wobbly – it will set as it cools.

8. Cool in the tin on a rack and then cover tightly and refrigerate overnight.

9. To serve, loosen the edge by running a knife around it and then unclip and remove the tin. Delicious served in slender slices with extra pouring cream and some soft fruit.

Simple Chocolate Mousse

Method

1. Put the chocolate and coffee into a heatproof bowl, stand the bowl over a pan of simmering water and leave until the chocolate has melted. Once melted stir thoroughly.

2. Separate the eggs and beat the yolks into the chocolate mixture.

3. Whisk the egg whites to stiff peaks. Fold into the chocolate mixture a third at a time until no white streaks can be seen.

4. Spoon into pretty glasses then chill in the fridge for a couple of hours or longer.

5. Serve with single cream, as a special treat, or decorate with chocolate shavings and fresh raspberries (pictured).

Ingredients

Serves 4

100g 70% dark chocolate

4 eggs, separated

2 tbsp of strong coffee (instant is fine)

Chocolate Pots

Method

1. Slowly heat the cream, then add the broken chocolate. Stir until melted.

2. Add the butter and stir until incorporated, followed by the egg yolks.

3. Divide between four ramekins, cover and chill in the fridge until set.

4. Makes an elegant desert served with soft fruit.

Ingredients

Serves 4

300ml single cream

200g 70% dark chocolate, broken into pieces

20g butter

2 egg yolks, lightly beaten

Banana Churros with Peanut & Caramel Dipping Sauce

Ingredients

Serves 4

For the sauce:
100g brown sugar
100ml double cream
20g butter
½ tsp vanilla extract
½ jar peanut butter

For the fritters:
300g self-raising flour
400ml boiling water
2 tbsp oil
1 large, ripe banana

Oil for deep frying,
heated to 180°C
Icing sugar for dusting

Method

1. Make the sauce first. Put the butter, double cream and brown sugar in a small saucepan and slowly bring to the boil. Reduce heat and simmer for two minutes, stirring occasionally.

2. Add the vanilla and simmer for another minute. Remove from the heat and allow to cool for five minutes. Whisk in the peanut butter and 2 tablespoons of boiling water. Set aside.

3. Put the flour in a large mixing bowl.

4. Mash the banana as smoothly as possible and blend with the boiling water and the oil.

5. Start pouring the banana mixture into the flour and use a large fork to gradually incorporate all the flour. You may not need all the banana mixture or you may need a little extra milk, it depends on the flour. You are looking for a very thick, sticky batter.

6. Spoon the batter into a piping bag fitted with a large nozzle, then, holding the bag over the pan of oil, squeeze out short lengths of batter – I find it easiest to squeeze with one hand and use the other to snip off lengths with a pair of kitchen scissors. If you don't want to use a piping bag you can drop small spoonsful of batter into the pan instead. Fry the fritters until they are a deep golden brown on all sides then drain thoroughly on some kitchen paper.

7. Serve immediately, dusted with icing sugar and with the dipping sauce alongside.

just bananas

 Bananas have been a fair trade favourite since they first appeared on our shelves over a decade ago, with over a billion fair trade bananas sold in the UK every year.

We peel, munch and bake our way through over £550 million worth of our favourite fruity snack each year.

But did you know that as well as growing upside down (who knew?) only one in three bananas in UK shops is sold as fair trade. Even though demand for the humble banana makes it worth billions worldwide, not everyone enjoys the benefits of the banana boom. There is huge competition in our supermarkets to sell us the cheapest bananas they can, so they pile 'em high and sell 'em cheap. Their huge buying power can keep prices really low for farmers.

When you buy a fair trade banana you can be sure that farmers were paid a fair price, with a guaranteed income that covers their cost of living and the cost of producing their crop.

Fair trade means safe working, and extra money to spend in the community on health, education and training.

Crops have been grown with respect for the environment, and there's no child labour.

If the banana you buy isn't fair trade, the workers who grew and harvested them may have worked long hours in poor and unsafe conditions, and received a price or wage so low that it's hard for them to put food on their table.

Banana farmers don't want charity. They just want a fair reward for their hard work. Your choice can really make a difference. So when you buy bananas, make sure they've got the Fairtrade mark.

'Magic' Lemon Pudding

This is one of those clever but oh-so-easy puddings which make a lovely light sponge top with a lemony sauce underneath. If you like lemon and ginger, add a teaspoon of ground ginger to the flour before adding to the mix instead of walnuts or sultanas.

Method

1. Preheat oven 180°C/gas mark 4.

2. Grease a 1 litre ovenproof dish.

3. Put the butter and sugar in a large mixing bowl and beat until light and fluffy. Add the lemon zest and juice, then beat in the egg yolks one at a time.

4. Add the flour and the milk and briefly beat until you have a smooth batter. It may look a little curdled but that's nothing to worry about. Stir in the walnuts or sultanas if using.

5. Whisk the egg whites until stiff and fold into the lemon batter. Pour the batter into the greased ovenproof dish.

6. Place dish in a roasting tin and pour enough boiling water into the tin to come halfway up the side of the dish.

7. Bake for 50-60 minutes, until the top is brown and feels slightly springy to the touch when lightly pressed.

8. Serve immediately with a little pouring cream.

Ingredients
Serves 6

50g butter or margarine

200g caster sugar

Zest of 1 lemon

100ml lemon juice (approximately 2 lemons)

3 eggs separated

50g plain flour

250ml milk

50g chopped walnuts/50g sultanas (optional)

Sticky Date Pudding with Toffee Sauce

Ingredients

Serves 6-8

120g dates, chopped

240ml water

1½ tsp bicarbonate of soda

90g butter

90g caster sugar

90g flour

3 eggs

1½ tsp baking powder

1½ tsp vanilla

Toffee sauce:

200g brown sugar

200ml double cream

40g butter

1 tsp vanilla

Method

1. Preheat oven to 180°C/gas mark 4.

2. Put the dates and water in a small saucepan and bring to the boil. Remove from the heat and stir in the bicarbonate of soda. Leave to cool.

3. Put the butter, caster sugar, eggs, flour, baking powder and vanilla into a food processor and blitz until combined. Add the date mixture and pulse a couple of times until evenly mixed.

4. Pour the batter into a shallow, greased baking dish and bake for 25-30 minutes or until the centre springs back when pressed gently with the back of your finger.

5. While the pudding bakes make the toffee sauce. Put all the ingredients into a pan and bring slowly to the boil, then simmer for two minutes.

6. Once cooked, remove the pudding from the oven and use a skewer or large fork to poke holes all over the pudding. Pour over half of the toffee sauce and serve the rest alongside.

7. A real treat served with some single cream too.

Toffee Grapes

These make a beautiful and unusual addition to a cheese board.
They go particularly well with a good blue cheese.

Method

1. Tip the sugar into a small saucepan and add the water. Bring to the boil over a medium heat, stirring to help dissolve the sugar. Once the sugar has dissolved add the vinegar and golden syrup.

2. If you have a sugar thermometer boil the mixture until it reaches 140°C or the 'hard crack' stage. If you don't have a thermometer you can test the toffee by pouring a little into a bowl of cold water. It should harden instantly and, when removed, be brittle. Start testing it once it is a deep bronze colour. If you can still squish the toffee it will need to cook for longer.

3. While the toffee is boiling pull the grapes from the stalks and insert a cocktail stick into the other end of the grape. If you prefer you can snip off bunches of two or three grapes and use the stalk to dip them with instead.

4. Once the toffee is ready, remove the pan from the heat and wait until it stops bubbling and begins to thicken slightly.

5. Working quickly and confidently, dip each grape into the toffee turning to coat evenly. Take care, it's hot! Lift up and allow any excess toffee to drip back into the pan, then stand on the baking parchment. As you work, the toffee will cool and thicken, if it becomes too thick pop it back over a low heat for a few seconds.

6. Once the grapes are coated, eat immediately, the toffee will harden very quickly but then start to liquidise if left for any length of time.

Ingredients

Makes approx 24

Seedless grapes - red, white or a mixture of the two
cocktail sticks
baking parchment
200g golden caster sugar
50ml water
½ tsp vinegar
2 tbsp golden syrup

Tasty tips

If grapes don't appeal try using apple slices or clementine segments instead.

Honeyed Pear Pie

Recipe donated by Helen Falconer-Flint

This is one of those recipes I know so well and make so often that it doesn't matter that I lost the 'written-down' version years ago. I can bake it from memory!

Ingredients

Serves 6-8

750g small, ripe pears, peeled, halved and cores removed

3 tbsp runny honey

Juice of half a lemon

50g walnuts very finely chopped

Finely grated zest of half an orange

200g plain flour

75g caster sugar

100g butter

1 beaten egg

Method

1. Preheat oven to 200°C/gas mark 6.

2. Put the pears in a saucepan, cover with cold water and add honey and lemon juice. Simmer gently for 10-15 minutes then allow to cool in the syrup.

3. Sieve flour into mixing bowl, rub in the butter, then stir in sugar, walnuts and orange zest.

4. Add the egg and combine to make a soft dough, cover and chill for 20 minutes.

5. Roll out two thirds of the pastry and line a 23cm pie dish and trim the edges.

6. Remove the pears from the syrup and arrange in the bottom of the dish.

7. Roll out the remainder of the pastry and use to cover the pie. Crimp the edges to seal and make a small hole in the centre to allow the steam to escape.

8. Brush the top with beaten egg and sprinkle with sugar.

9. Bake for 35 minutes till golden brown.

Mincemeat & Frangipane Tart

Method

1. Preheated oven 160°C/gas mark 3.

2. Line a 20cm loose bottomed flan tin with the pastry and spoon over the mincemeat.

3. Beat the ground almonds, butter and sugar together to make a paste then beat in the eggs. Spread the frangipane mixture over the mincemeat and cover completely.

4. Bake for 30 minutes or until the frangipane is golden brown and springs back when pressed lightly with a finger.

Ingredients
Serves 6

200g shortcrust pastry

4 heaped tbsp mincemeat

100g ground almonds

100g golden caster sugar

100g softened butter

½ tsp almond extract

2 eggs

The people behind the products
Sher Ghazi, Mountain Fruits, Pakistan

"Local markets are important, but getting a fair trade deal for fruit farmers in these remote valleys is a lifeline."

Baklava

Ingredients

Makes approx 30 small pieces

1 pack filo pastry
50g butter, melted
75g walnuts
75g shelled
  pistachio nuts

Syrup:

30g raw cane sugar
½ tsp ground
  cinnamon
250ml water
300g granulated
  sugar
3 strips of lemon
  zest peeled from
  a lemon
5 cardamom pods,
  bashed with a
  rolling pin

Method

1. Preheat the oven to 180°C/gas mark 4. Grease a 18cm square tin.

2. Make the syrup. Put all the ingredients into a pan and stir over a low heat. Once the sugar has dissolved bring the pan to the boil and then simmer until you have a nice glossy syrup. Remove the lemon and cardamom and leave to cool.

3. Toast the nuts on a baking tray in the oven for a few minutes, until they smell fragrant, making sure they don't burn. Tip them onto a board and chop finely. Put in a bowl and mix with the raw cane sugar and ground cinnamon.

4. Unroll the filo pastry and cut in half across the centre fold to make 16 square sheets. Take one sheet and lay in the greased tin, scrunching any excess into the sides and corners. Using a pastry brush lightly spread a small amount of butter over the pastry then place another sheet on top and brush with butter. Do this twice more then scatter a thin layer of the nut mixture over the pastry. Repeat the 4 layers of pastry topped with nuts twice more and finish with 4 layers of pastry on the top.

5. Place the tin in the freezer for 15 minutes, this will allow the butter to set and make cutting it easier. Then use a small sharp knife to cut in a criss-cross pattern making small diamond shapes into the top of the pastry. Try to make the cuts about three quarters of the way through but not right to the bottom layers.

6. Bake in the preheated oven for 20 minutes then decrease the heat to 130°C/gas mark 2 and cook for another 30-40 minutes until the top is golden brown and the pastry has puffed up. Remove from the oven and pour over half the syrup. Allow this to be absorbed before pouring over the remaining syrup. Leave to stand for at least 12 hours before cutting and serving. Store uncovered to avoid the pastry going soggy.

Sugar farmer Alfred Butao
Photo: Richard Else

sweet justice

Ever wondered if your fair trade purchase really makes a difference? Just ask Alfred.

Kasinthula Cane Growers in Malawi were the first growers in Africa to produce fair trade sugar. Traidcraft was there at the very start, working to help them gain Fairtrade certification, and we bought the very first fair trade sugar they produced. Now, Kasinthula is a huge success story, and their fair trade sugar is used in many fair trade products you can buy on the high street.

Fair trade has really made a difference to the farmers who grow sugar cane here on small plots of just a couple of hectares.

The extra income that fair trade brings has paid for medicines for the local clinic, higher yielding cane plants, and boreholes providing sweet, clean and safe water for hundreds of people in two local villages.

Farmers like Alfred Butao have experienced for themselves the good things that fair trade brings to family life, every day.

"Now we are able to buy cooking oil and meat so we have a balanced diet. I am able to feed my children."

In Malawi, primary school is free but parents try to send their children to private schools to get a better education.

"My elder child goes to private school and I have to pay for him. It would be impossible for me to pay the school fees without growing sugar. Now, because of sugar, each and every month I have money."

Alfred's village now receives electricity. Electric light means his children can study after school, and he and his wife Rose can use their radio, "We like to listen to music and the news."

The benefits are clear, but still, less than one percent of the world's sugar cane is fair trade certified.

"The extra for fair trade on one item may be small, but if lots of people pay a little bit extra it makes a big difference for us. I would be so happy if our whole volume of sugar that we are producing could be sold at a fair trade price." Alfred Butao.

biscuits

Crispy, crumbly or downright dunkable, these homemade biscuits are hard to resist - and great sellers on a cake stall!

Choc Chunk Cookies

These are a real favourite with people who love fair trade chocolate. We received lots of chocolate cookie recipes, and this one combines the best of them all.

Method

1. Preheat oven to 180°C/gas mark 4.

2. Line 2-3 baking sheets.

3. Melt 100g of the dark chocolate in a heatproof bowl over a pan of simmering water.

4. Stir in the sugar, butter, peanut butter, egg and vanilla, beating well with a wooden spoon until well mixed.

5. Stir in the flour, the milk chocolate chunks, the peanuts and another 100g of the dark chocolate chunks. The mixture will be quite soft.

6. Drop large spoonfuls in about 12 piles onto the baking sheets, leaving spreading room. Stick 2-3 pieces of remaining chocolate onto the top of each cookie.

7. Bake for 12-15 minutes until they darken slightly at the edges.

8. Transfer carefully to a wire rack, they crisp up as they cool.

Ingredients

Makes 8-10 cookies

300g dark chocolate, roughly chopped

100g milk chocolate, roughly chopped

100g light muscovado sugar

85g butter or margarine

100g crunchy peanut butter

1 medium egg, beaten

½ tsp vanilla extract

100g self-raising flour

100g salted peanuts

bake a difference

"The education of our children matters to us, and it is important for us to see them in school."
Bai Koffe Leon, Cocoa farmer, Cote D'Ivoire

Beanies Cookies

Lots of people donated versions of this popular recipe!

Ingredients

Makes 8-10 cookies

100g butter
  or margarine
100g light muscovado
  sugar
1 tbsp golden syrup
150g self-raising flour
3 packets of chocolate
  beanies

Method

1. Preheat oven 180°C/gas mark 4.

2. Beat together the butter and sugar until light and creamy, then beat in the golden syrup.

3. Work in half the flour, then stir in the other half along with two packets of the beanies, working the dough together with your fingers. Divide into 10-15 balls depending on what size you want the biscuits to be.

4. Place well apart on baking sheets and decorate with the remaining beanies.

5. Bake for 12-15 minutes until golden. Allow to cool for 5 minutes, then transfer to a cooling rack. They will crisp up as they cool.

When I sell biscuits on a stall, the ones marked fair trade always go first!

Honey & Apple Biscuits

Recipe donated by Sylvia Harris

These are great favourites with my grandchildren, who absolutely love picking up the windfall apples, then making and eating these biscuits.

Method

1. Preheat oven to 180°C/gas mark 4.

2. Line a baking sheet with baking parchment.

3. Chop the apples, skins, pips and all, and put with water in a pan, heat and simmer until the apple has broken down. Sieve the apple sauce through a fine mesh leaving only the seeds and skin behind. You will need 150ml of the apple pulp for the biscuits.

4. Cream the butter in a bowl till soft. Mix in the flour until smooth before adding the sugar.

5. Mix in the apple purée then add all other ingredients and mix well.

6. Drop tablespoons of the batter onto the lined baking sheet, setting them at least 5cm apart then press a slice of almond into the top of each one.

7. Bake for 12-15 minutes, or until golden brown. Cool on the baking tray for 10 minutes then transfer to a wire rack.

8. Keeps for seven days in an airtight tin.

Ingredients

Makes approx. 12

300g apples
300ml water
80g wholemeal flour
80g butter
100g muscavado sugar
1 tbsp runny honey
½ tsp baking powder
pinch of salt
blanched almonds
  chopped lengthways

Chunky Chocolate Orange & Ginger Cookies

Recipe donated by Val Rudd
Just try these and you'll see why I chose them!

Ingredients
Makes 14-18

250g butter
  or margarine

50g caster sugar

100g light muscovado
  sugar

300g self-raising flour

2 tbsp milk

2 x 100g bars
  dark chocolate with
  orange and ginger,
  roughly chopped

50g walnuts,
  roughly chopped

Method

1. Preheat oven to 180°C/gas mark 4. Line 2-3 baking sheets.

2. Beat together butter and both sugars until fluffy and light.

3. Stir in flour and milk, mixing well, then stir in the chocolate and walnuts.

4. Divide into approximately 14-18 balls (depending on the size of cookie preferred) and place on the baking sheets. Flatten slightly with your fingertips. Allow room for spreading.

5. Bake for 15-20 minutes until golden. Cool for 5 minutes then transfer to a wire rack.

Hannah's Fork Biscuits

Recipe donated by Dumfries Fairtrade Group
These sell really well on a cake stall!

Method

1. Preheat oven to 180°C/gas mark 4. Lightly grease two largish baking trays.

2. Put the butter in a bowl and beat to soften. Gradually beat in the sugar and then add the flour and cocoa together.

3. Bring the mixture together with your hands to form a dough – it may seem quite dry and crumbly at this stage. Form the dough into little balls about the size of a walnut and place well apart on the baking trays. Press them down with a fork.

4. Bake in the oven for 15-20 minutes. Lift off the baking tray and leave to cool.

5. Make some white icing with water and drizzle over them in random patterns.

Ingredients
Makes 12

200g softened butter
100g caster sugar
285g self-raising flour
15g cocoa
Icing sugar to decorate

These biscuits are delicately flavoured so you could swap up to 30g of the flour for cocoa if you wanted to.

Almond Shorties

Recipe donated by Tracy Mitchell

Ingredients
Makes 30

100g butter
50g golden caster sugar
100g ground almonds
1 egg yolk
½ tsp vanilla extract
½ tsp salt
175g self-raising flour

Method

1. Preheat oven to 180°C/gas mark 4.

2. Line a large baking sheet.

3. Put the almonds into a food processor and pulse until finely ground.

4. Cream the butter and sugar until soft and light in colour. Add the nuts, egg yolk, vanilla, salt and sifted flour and mix to a dough.

5. Work the dough into 2 x 15cm rolls, wrap in clingfilm and chill for 20 minutes. Remove from fridge and cut each roll into 1cm discs and put them on the prepared baking tray.

6. Bake for 10-15 minutes until just golden.

7. Remove from oven, leave to harden for 5 minutes, then cool on rack. Store in an airtight tin.

Biscotti

Recipe donated by Dumfries Fairtrade Group
Ideal for dunking in your fair trade coffee!

Ingredients
Makes 12 slices

200g plain flour

1 tsp baking powder

80g golden caster sugar

50g desiccated coconut
  (or ground almonds)

100g mixed fruit

80g glacé cherries, halved

30g nuts such as
  almonds, brazils or
  cashews roughly
  chopped

2 eggs, beaten

Method

1. Preheat oven to 180°C/gas mark 4.

2. Line two baking trays.

3. In a large bowl mix together the flour, baking powder, caster sugar, coconut (or ground almonds), mixed fruit, cherries, and nuts.

4. Gradually add the eggs and mix until a dough forms, using your hands to combine if necessary. If the dough is too wet add a little more flour.

5. Shape the dough into a log and place on a lined baking sheet, flattening a little until approximately 4cm thick and 20-25cm long.

6. Bake for 25minutes. Remove from the oven and reduce the temperature to 160°C/gas mark 3.

7. Let the dough cool for about 10 minutes, then use a serrated knife and cut at an angle into 3cm slices.

8. Place on the trays and return to the oven for 20 minutes to dry out. Allow to cool completely.

9. Serve with a cup of coffee (and dunk!).

gift food

Everyone loves a homemade
foodie gift - what a treat!
Here are some ideas for
every occasion.

Traidcraft Mincemeat

Method

1. Make sure all of the dried fruits are finely chopped to around the same size.

2. In a large bowl, mix the first nine ingredients together until well combined. It is easiest to do this with your hands.

3. Dissolve the sugar in the brandy, rum or apple juice and add to the mixture. Cover and leave in a cool place overnight.

4. Stir the mixture thoroughly before packing into sterile jars. Leave for a month to mature before using.

Ingredients

Makes approximately
3 x 500g jars

500g dried mixed fruit

300g other dried fruit of choice – apricots, mango, pear etc

250g cooking apples, peeled and finely chopped

125g slivered almonds

125g suet

grated zest of 1 lemon

grated zest of 1 orange

½ tsp of cinnamon

¼ tsp of nutmeg

¼ tsp of allspice

250g dark brown soft sugar

250ml brandy, dark rum or apple juice (if preferred)

The people behind the products
Parvarti Jadhav, Fruit Grower

A farmer for over 25 years, Parvarti grows vine fruits for sultanas, and is a board member for her local grower's association in India. One of four women in an organisation of 100 farmers, she works hard to encourage other women to join her.

"With fair trade we have hygienic conditions, there is no child labour and, for the same job, the same salary for men and women. Fair business."

Emergency Cake Jars

Sometimes, when friends are in need of comfort... only cake will do!

Ingredients
Makes 3 jars

150g self-raising flour
150g butter
150g caster sugar
3 eggs
100g butter
200g icing sugar
jam
raspberries

You will need:
3 jam jars or similar

A thoughtful gift when presented in a pretty jar with a shiny spoon and handmade label.

Method

1. Preheat oven to 180°C/gas mark 4.

2. Put the first four ingredients into a food mixer or food processor and mix until you have a smooth cake batter.

3. Spoon into a greased and base lined tin 33 x 20cm and bake for 30 minutes until golden and the cake springs back when pressed lightly with your finger. Cool in the tin for 5 minutes then turn out onto a wire rack and allow to cool completely.

4. Beat the butter and icing sugar together until you have a light and full buttercream.

5. Using a 5cm biscuit cutter, stamp out 9 rounds of cake and carefully ease one round into the bottom of each jar.

6. Using a spoon or piping bag, top each round of cake with some jam and then some buttercream. Repeat with another round of cake then jam and butter cream. Place the final round of cake on top. Dust with icing sugar and decorate with fresh raspberries.

7. Place the lids on the jars and decorate.

8. Cake must be stored in the fridge and used within 2 days.

9. To make a chocolate version replace 2 tablespoons of flour with 2 tablespoons of cocoa powder and add a tablespoon of cocoa powder to the icing sugar to make the buttercream. For a lemon version add the finely grated zest of a lemon to the cake mixture and use lemon curd instead of jam.

Orange Chutney

Ingredients

Makes 4 x 450g jars

4 large oranges

2 large eating apples

1 large onion

100g stem ginger,
  finely chopped

½ tsp dried
  crushed chillis

500g light
  muscovado sugar

100g raisins

500ml vinegar

1 tsp salt

½ tsp pepper

Method

1. Peel the oranges, removing all the white pith and any pips, then chop roughly. Peel, core and chop the apples. Peel and chop the onion.

2. Put all the ingredients into a large pan and simmer gently until thick, approximately 1 hour.

3. Use a jam funnel to transfer the chutney into hot, sterilised jars and seal.

4. Allow to mature for two weeks before eating.

Tregassick Tomato Chutney

Recipe donated by Isabel Teague

Method

1. Place all the ingredients into a large stainless steel saucepan and heat gently until the sugar has completely dissolved.

2. Bring to the boil, stirring, then simmer on a low heat, stirring regularly (to make sure the mixture does not burn on the bottom of the pan) for about 1 hour or until thick and pulpy.

3. Use a jam funnel to pour the chutney into hot sterilised jars and cover.

4. Store the jars in a cool dark place for 2 weeks before eating.

Ingredients
Makes 4 x 450g jars

1 kg tomatoes, peeled and chopped
200g onions, chopped
100g sultanas
250g apples, peeled, cored and coarsely chopped
300g raw cane sugar
200ml vinegar
2 tsp salt
½ tsp ground allspice
½ tsp ground ginger
½ tsp ground black pepper
1 tsp cayenne pepper
1 tsp black onion seeds

Apricot & Walnut Preserve

Method

1. Put the apricots and water into a bowl and soak overnight.

2. Slice one orange thinly, squeeze the juice from the second orange and the lemon.

3. Put all the ingredients, except the walnuts, into a large saucepan, bring to the boil and then simmer until the mixture is thick and the fruit looks transparent. Stir in the walnuts.

4. Use a jam funnel to transfer the preserve into hot, sterilised jars then seal, label and store in a cool dark place for two weeks before using.

Ingredients
Makes 2 x 450g jars

500g dried apricots
2 oranges
100g raisins
1 litre water
1 lemon
250g chopped walnuts
500g raw cane sugar

Scottish Tablet

Recipe donated by Margaret McGowan

This Scottish sweet is usually served after meals with tea or coffee. It's great to sell at charity fairs or coffee mornings when attractively packaged, and can also be used as favours at weddings.

Ingredients

Makes approx
30 pieces

1kg granulated sugar
125g butter
500ml full fat milk
2 tbsp golden syrup
1 tsp vanilla essence

Method

1. Grease a shallow 20cm x 25cm baking tray that is at least 2.5cm deep. Set aside.

2. Clip a sugar thermometer onto a heavy-bottomed saucepan and add the sugar, butter, milk and syrup. Place over a moderate heat and stir until the ingredients have dissolved. Bring slowly to the boil and then boil hard until the mixture reaches 116°C/240F/soft ball.

3. Immediately remove from the heat, wait until bubbles subside then add the vanilla essence. Beat vigorously with a wooden spoon until the mixture changes its consistency and becomes thick, pale and creamy and starts to 'grain.'

4. Immediately pour into the greased tray and leave to cool. As soon as it begins to set, after about 20 minutes or more, cut the tablet into squares. Eat when cool.

savouries

Fair trade ingredients aren't just for baking!
Quinoa, lentils, rice, pasta and couscous
make fabulous quick and
tasty meals.

Clean Green Quinoa

Method

1. Put the rinsed quinoa in a pan and add the water. Bring to the boil and then simmer for approximately 20 minutes until tender and the germ has sprung away from the grain in little spirals. Drain thoroughly, cover with a lid and allow to rest in the pan.

2. After five minutes tip the quinoa into a large salad bowl and break up with two forks to loosen, then stir in the Thai curry paste. Leave to cool, tossing occasionally.

3. Steam the sugar snap peas until just tender then refresh under cold running water to keep the green colour. Drain well and pat dry with some kitchen paper.

4. Stir all the green vegetables into the quinoa and add lime juice to taste.

5. Serve decorated with a few slices of chilli, celery and lime zest and a tiny drizzle of olive oil.

Ingredients
Serves 2

- 100g quinoa, rinsed thoroughly under running water
- 200ml water
- 1 tsp Thai green curry paste
- 100g sugar snap peas or mangetout
- 1 bunch of spring onions, green part only
- 1 stick of celery
- ½ small green chilli
- juice and zest of 1 lime
- olive oil to taste

The people behind the products
Mahmoud al Quadi, Olive Farmer

In the West Bank farming village of Beni Zeid, fair trade is improving livelihoods and inspiring community change. Mahmoud hopes that the next generation can profit too.

"Because of fair trade we are thinking collectively now. We don't just develop for ourselves, we're developing a community."

Coconut Rice & Chicken

Recipe donated by Tracy Mitchell
A tasty one-bowl treat.

Ingredients

Serves 4

300g basmati rice

4 chicken breasts

2 tbsp sunflower oil

1 large onion, peeled and chopped

1 tsp garlic paste

1 thumb sized piece of ginger

1 small chilli, deseeded and finely chopped

400g can of chopped tomatoes

2 tbsp of fresh coriander, chopped

3 peppers, mixed colours, finely chopped

half a 400ml can coconut milk

freshly ground pepper

Method

1. Rinse the rice and cook according to instructions on the packet.

2. Put the chicken breasts in a pan and just cover with water. Bring to the boil and simmer for 10-12 minutes until the chicken juices run clear when tested with a knife. Allow to cool and cut into cubes or slices.

3. Heat 1 tablespoon of oil in a wok or large frying pan and cook the chopped onion slowly with the garlic, ginger and chilli until the onion is soft, but not brown.

4. Add the tomatoes, bring to the boil and simmer and reduce until thick. Add the chopped coriander and cook briefly. Remove the sauce from the heat and put it in a bowl.

5. Add the rest of the oil to the washed frying pan and stir fry the peppers for 2-3 minutes. Add the coconut milk. Stir well, then add the tomato sauce, cooked rice and chicken.

6. Return to the hob, heat thoroughly, stirring all the time.

7. Decorate with extra coriander and serve.

Tomato & Mozzarella Pasta

Method

1. Preheat oven to 220°C/gas mark 8.

2. Put the cherry tomatoes, courgette, onion and olive oil into a bowl and toss together until everything is coated with oil.

3. Tip into an oven tray and spread out evenly, then roast in the preheated oven for 20 minutes or until the vegetables are soft, tender and browning at the edges.

4. While the vegetables are roasting cook the pasta in a large pan of salted boiling water for 11-13 minutes, until cooked to your liking. Drain.

5. Mix together the vegetables and pasta adding the torn mozzarella and the balsamic vinegar to taste. Sprinkle with finely sliced basil and serve.

Ingredients
Serves 4

500g cherry tomatoes

1 courgette, sliced thinly

1 small onion, halved and sliced thinly

2 balls of mozzarella, torn into pieces

2 tbsp olive oil

1 tbsp balsamic vinegar (optional)

400g dried pasta

basil leaves

Tasty tips
Great served at room temperature as part of a buffet.

Cashew Nut Curry

Recipe donated by Helen Wallis

I made this vegetarian curry dish for a fair trade cooking competition when I worked in the design studio at Traidcraft nearly twenty years ago. It's the only competition I've ever won, so I'm delighted to have the chance to brag about it all over again!

Ingredients

Serves 4

250g cashew nuts,
50g desiccated coconut
1 tsp coriander seeds
1 tsp poppy seeds
1 tsp ground cumin
½ tsp tumeric
1 red chilli, deseeded and finely chopped
2 tbsp oil
6 celery sticks
2 onions
2 tbsp garlic and ginger paste (or three crushed garlic cloves and a tbsp of grated ginger)
1 large courgette
1 green pepper
300ml vegetable stock
tin of tomatoes, chopped
salt and pepper to taste.

To garnish: shredded coriander leaves

Method

1. Place the coconut, coriander, poppy seeds, cumin, tumeric and chilli in a pestle and mortar, and crush (alternatively use an electric blender adding a tablespoon of oil.)

2. Heat the oil in a pan, add the celery and onions and sauté for 5 minutes, until just coloured. Add the courgette, pepper, garlic and ginger paste, the ground spices and cashews and cook for 5 minutes, stirring regularly.

3. Add the stock and bring to the boil, then add the tomatoes and cover and simmer for 30 minutes. Season to taste.

4. To serve, sprinkle the curry with the shredded coriander.

Tasty tips
Delicious served with a cucumber and yogurt raita.

Malawi Toor Dhal & Potato Soup

Ingredients

Serves 4

100g toor dhal, rinsed and drained

small piece of fresh ginger, chopped

300g potatoes, peeled and diced

1 tsp garlic puree

1 large onion, peeled and sliced

½ small chilli, deseeded and finely chopped

1 litre of vegetable stock

salt and pepper

1 tbsp of coriander, chopped

Recipe donated by Tracey Mitchell

Method

1. Put the dhal and ginger in a pan and add the potato, garlic, onion, chilli and stock. Bring to the boil and cover. Simmer until the dhal is soft (about 30 minutes).

2. Season to taste. Put the mixture into a food processor or use a stick blender to blend until smooth, adding extra stock if required until the soup reaches desired consistency.

3. Return the soup to the pan and reheat over a low heat, stirring continuously.

4. Serve in a warm bowl with a sprinkling of coriander.

Sweet Potato Fritters

Recipe donated by Dumfries Fairtrade Group

Method

1. Put the dry ingredients into a bowl, whisk in the egg and milk to make a coating batter.

2. Put 2cm of oil in a large pan and heat to 180°C.

3. Dip the slices of potato into the batter and fry, turning occasionally, until a deep golden brown on both sides.

4. Drain on kitchen paper and sprinkle with chopped parsley before serving.

5. Makes approximately 16 fritters.

Ingredients
Makes approx 16

2 tbsp plain flour
1 tbsp desiccated coconut
1 tbsp caster sugar
1 tsp sesame seeds
1 tsp black onion seeds
½ tsp salt
½ tsp paprika
1 egg
3 tbsp milk
1 large sweet potato, peeled and thinly sliced

Carbonara Frittata

Ingredients

Serves 4

150g cooked pasta

1 tbsp olive oil

100g smoked bacon, chopped

1 small onion, finely sliced

4 eggs, beaten

50g finely grated parmesan cheese

100ml double cream

50g frozen peas

finely chopped parsley for garnish

Method

1. Preheat grill on high setting with the shelf on the middle runners.

2. Heat the oil in a large non-stick frying pan over a medium heat. Add the smoked bacon and fry briskly until it begins to brown around the edges then add the onion.

3. In a large bowl whisk the eggs, cream and parmesan cheese together. Once the bacon and onion are golden brown remove from the pan with a slotted spoon and add to the egg and cream mixture along with the peas and pasta. Stir everything together thoroughly.

4. Pour the mixture back into the frying pan and cook over a medium heat until the base has set and is beginning to colour. Transfer the pan to the grill and continue cooking until the frittata has set in the middle and the top is golden brown.

5. Serve cut into wedges.

Thai Green Curry

Method

1. Put all the paste ingredients in a food processor or stick blender goblet and blitz until you have a smooth paste. You can add a tablespoon or so of water to help it along if necessary.

2. Pour the coconut milk into a wok or wide sauté pan and bring to the boil.

3. Stir in the paste then add the diced chicken and the vegetables and simmer until the chicken is cooked through.

4. Serve with basmati rice and garnish with extra fresh coriander and grated lime zest.

Ingredients
Serves 4

For the paste:

2 garlic cloves, peeled

2 inch piece of fresh ginger, peeled and chopped

2 chillies, seeds removed if milder result preferred

2 shallots, peeled and chopped

1 pack each of fresh mint, fresh basil and fresh coriander

zest & juice of 1 lime

1tsp turmeric

1tsp ground cumin

1tsp ground coriander

1tsp black peppercorns

1tbsp fish sauce

1tbsp soy sauce

For the curry:

tin of coconut milk

4 chicken breast fillets, diced

100g mange tout

100g fine green beans

Chicken Korma

Ingredients

Serves 2-3

500g boneless chicken breast cut into chunks

100g almonds

100g cashew nuts

150ml full fat yoghurt

150ml double cream

1 large green chilli, finely chopped (seeds removed if milder result preferred)

1 inch fresh ginger, finely grated

½ tsp salt

1 cinnamon stick

3 bay leaves

5 each black peppercorns, cloves, cardamom pods

½ tsp turmeric

½ tsp chilli powder

1 tsp sweet paprika

2 tsp ground coriander

flaked coconut, toasted (optional)

chopped mint leaves (optional)

Method

1. Prepare the nuts. Put the cashew nuts in a bowl and cover with cold water. Place the almonds in a small heatproof bowl and cover with boiling water.

2. Once the water has cooled drain and remove the skins from the almonds, they should slip off quite easily. Drain the cashew nuts.

3. Put the nuts in a blender along with 100-150ml of cold water and blitz to a paste. Scrape this paste into a large pan.

4. Add the yoghurt, cream, chilli, ginger, salt and all the spices. Stir to mix.

5. Add the chicken and stir to coat.

6. Bring to a simmer over a medium heat, stirring occasionally. Continue to simmer until the chicken is cooked through.

7. Serve garnished with toasted coconut and mint leaves.

Parmesan, Stilton & Walnut Crackers

Ingredients

Makes 30 plus crackers

200g parmesan
250g walnut halves
125g Stilton

Method

1. Pre-heat oven to 200°C/gas mark 6.

2. Line baking trays with baking parchment.

3. Chop the parmesan into rough chunks, then blitz in a food processor until it is fine crumbs.

4. Tip in the walnuts and blitz again until chopped roughly.

5. Crumble in the Stilton and pulse for a second or two to blend.

6. Using a dessert spoon pile the mixture onto the baking trays. Leave a good margin between each one as they will spread out as they cook. Bake in the oven until the crackers are deep golden brown around the edges.

7. Remove from the oven and allow to cool slightly before lifting carefully and moving to a cooling rack. Allow to cool completely.

8. They will keep for several days in an airtight container.

Traidcraft. A fair trade swap for your supermarket shop

Fair trade food. These days, it's a billion pound industry with a wide range of brands and goods to choose from.

So people often ask us, 'why should we buy our fair trade groceries from Traidcraft?'

Well, it's all about our connections.

You connect directly with small-scale producers, the communities who will simply never be reached by bigger companies or supermarket buyers.

You walk hand-in-hand with those farmers as they trade their way out of poverty.

You support fair and just supply chains that value and respect the people and places that are part of them.

You support a socially responsible business which puts people before profit.

The basic principles of fair trade were to change the way trade works for the poor. To help vulnerable farmers and artisans to find a market for their food and crafts, and trade their own way out of poverty.

We've come a long way. But bigger companies still control more than 70% of world trade. For big business, trade, even fair trade, will always be about the bottom line.

Traidcraft is different. For us, justice, fairness and dignity are fundamental to the way we work. We do the things that supermarkets and big businesses don't. Or can't. Or won't.

We're a small company that makes a big difference.

Because fair trade isn't just a part of our business. It's ALL of our business, and we're 100% committed to it.

Find out more about Traidcraft's work at www.traidcraft.co.uk.

Shop online for our quality food and crafts at www.traidcraftshop.co.uk

Pesto & Quinoa Stuffed Peppers

Ingredients

Serves 2

100g quinoa
2 large red peppers
2 tbsp olive oil
1 onion, finely sliced
1 stick of celery,
  finely sliced
chopped chives for
  garnish

For Feta filling:

200g Feta cheese,
  crumbled
20 black olives,
  roughly chopped
fresh parsley,
  finely chopped
Seasoning

For Pesto filling:

6 heaped tbsp Brazil
  and Walnut pesto
  (see page 151)
1 onion, finely sliced
1 stick of celery,
  finely sliced
Seasoning

Method

1. Preheat oven to 190°C/gas mark 6.

2. Rinse the quinoa very thoroughly in a sieve under running water. Put into a pan with 150ml of water, bring to the boil then simmer gently until all the water has gone and the quinoa is tender.

3. Cut the peppers in half vertically through the stem. Remove the seeds and any membranes and lay cut side up in an ovenproof dish. Drizzle with a little olive oil. Roast in the oven until just tender but not to the point of collapse.

4. While the peppers are roasting fry the onion and celery in the remaining oil until softened and beginning to turn golden around the edges.

5. **If using the Feta cheese and olives:** add the onion mixture, Feta cheese, olives, parsley and seasoning to the quinoa and mix well then spoon into the pepper halves.

6. **If using the pesto:** add the onion mixture, pesto and seasoning to the quinoa and mix well, then spoon into the pepper halves.

7. Return the peppers to the oven and bake until the filling is piping hot and the tops are beginning to brown.

8. Garnish with chopped chives and serve with a crisp green salad.

Stuffed Marrow

Ingredients

Serves 4

1 medium sized marrow

1 tbsp olive oil

1 onion, chopped

1 green pepper, seeds removed and diced

250g pork shoulder, finely diced

1 tin chopped tomatoes

200ml water

1 tbsp tomato purée

125ml red wine

1 stock cube (pork, chicken or vegetable)

1 tsp fennel seeds

½ tsp crushed chilli flakes

150g pasta shapes

parsley for garnish

Method

1. Prepare the marrow. Trim the ends off the marrow and cut into four equal pieces. Use a small sharp knife to remove the seeds and soft centre from each piece of marrow then stand the pieces upright in a microwaveable dish. Sprinkle with a little salt and pour about 50mls of water into the dish. Cover tightly with clingfilm and set aside.

2. Heat the oil in a sauté pan and soften the onion and pepper. Add the pork to the pan and fry until golden brown.

3. Stir in the fennel seeds and crushed chilli then add the tinned tomatoes, red wine, water, stock cube and the tomato purée.

4. Bring to the boil then cover the pan and simmer over the lowest possible heat for an hour or until the pork is tender.

5. Add the pasta to the pan, bring up to the boil and cook until the pasta is al dente.

6. Meanwhile microwave* the marrow on high until it is tender when poked with the tip of a knife. Drain.

7. Spoon the pork and pasta mixture into and around the marrow pieces in the dish then garnish with parsley and serve.

*If you don't use a microwave the marrow can be steamed or baked until tender while the pork sauce is cooking.

Brazil & Walnut Pesto

Method

1. Put the nuts, basil, garlic, lemon zest and juice into a blender or food processor and whizz to a coarse purée.

2. Tip into a bowl and stir in the parmesan cheese then gradually add the olive oil until you have a spoonable dressing. Season to taste.

3. When serving with pasta it helps to save some of the cooking water from the pasta and add a few tablespoons to help make a nice coating sauce.

Ingredients
Serves 4-6

100g Brazil nuts

100g walnuts

2 large packs fresh basil, leaves only

2 garlic cloves

zest and juice of a lemon

50g grated parmesan

seasoning

50-75ml olive oil

bake a difference

"Your olive oil is quite simply the best I've ever tasted."

Thai Sweet Chilli Dipping Sauce

Ingredients

2 garlic cloves, peeled

5 long red chillies roughly chopped, membranes and seeds removed

100g caster sugar

100ml rice vinegar or white wine vinegar

100ml water

1 tbs fish sauce (optional)

Recipe donated by Lizzie White

One of the best things about a Meet the People Tour* is the opportunity to share in some delicious local food. When I think of the memorable meals I have enjoyed with local people when travelling, my tour to Thailand is always one of the first things I think about. Meals in Thailand are always sociable occasions, often with a number of shared dishes to choose from. Here's my favourite quick and easy recipe that always reminds me of Thailand.

Method

1. Put a small plate in freezer for testing – you will need this later to test! Put the chillies and the garlic in a spice grinder or in a mortar and pestle and grind to a paste.

2. Transfer the paste to a pan along with the sugar, vinegar and water (and fish sauce if using). Boil the mixture vigorously for 5 minutes until it starts to become syrupy.

3. Test the consistency by putting half a teaspoon of the sauce onto the cold plate. Keep boiling until you are happy with the consistency. If eating immediately allow to cool before serving. Or use a jam funnel to transfer to a hot, sterilised jar and seal.

Tasty tips

Now you just need to decide what to dip in it! Perfect with cucumber sticks, salads, crab cakes or try spicy little chicken balls - recipe overleaf.

* www.meetthepeople.skedaddle.co.uk

Spicy Chicken Balls

Ingredients

Makes approx. 30 balls

400g chicken breast fillet

2 spring onions,
  roughly chopped

2 garlic cloves, peeled

1 chilli, roughly chopped

1 handful fresh coriander,
  leaves and stems

1½ tbsp Thai curry paste
  (red or green)

25g creamed coconut

1 egg

100g salted peanuts

handful of green beans,
  roughly chopped

oil for deep frying

Method

1. Put everything but the peanuts and beans into a food processor and blitz to a paste. Add the beans and peanuts and pulse to combine.

2. Roll into walnut sized balls and deep fry until a deep golden brown. Drain on kitchen paper and serve with the chilli dipping sauce.

Pork & Leek Pasta

Method

1. Heat a wide, shallow pan and fry the pork mince briskly until it begins to brown. Add the leeks and continue frying until they have softened slightly.

2. Add the wine or stock and allow to bubble for a few minutes then add the spinach. It will gradually wilt down as you stir. Once the spinach has wilted, turn the heat to a low simmer and half cover the pan.

3. Cook the pasta in a large pan of boiling salted water for approximately 11-13 minutes, until done to your liking.

4. Drain the pasta and add to the meat mixture. Stir in the double cream and the cheese and allow to stand for two minutes.

5. Serve garnished with the chopped parsley.

Ingredients
Serves 4

500g minced pork
2 large leeks, sliced
250g spinach
100ml white wine
 or stock
50ml double cream
50g Stilton cheese
400g dried pasta
chopped parsley

Ghanaian Groundnut Soup

Recipe donated by Mark Cottier

I discovered groundnut soup when travelling in Ghana on a Meet the People Tour. This recipe uses the fabulous cheat of peanut butter to make a quick, easy soup with all of the taste of West Africa, bringing back some fabulous memories. Good in summer, and a really great winter warmer too with the fresh chilli and ginger!

Ingredients

serves 4

1 clove garlic, chopped

1 onion, chopped

1-2 tbsp finely grated ginger

1 tbsp tomato puree

1 tsp ground cumin

1 red pepper finely sliced

1 tbsp groundnut or sunflower oil

1 small red chilli, de-seeded and finely chopped

1 can chopped tomatoes (400g) or passata

3 tbsp peanut butter

500ml vegetable stock

pepper to taste

Method

1. Gently fry the ginger, cumin, garlic, onion and sliced red pepper in the oil for a few minutes until golden and the pepper is beginning to soften.

2. Add the chilli and tomato puree and fry for a further 2 minutes.

3. Add the tinned tomatoes and peanut butter, stir through and bring to the boil and simmer for 5 minutes.

4. Add stock to preferred taste and consistency.

5. You can blend the soup before or after adding the peanut butter depending upon how smooth you would like it to be.

Quinoa Flatbreads

Recipe donated by Patricia White

One of the unexpected delights of my tour of Peru was the amazing food we enjoyed throughout the trip. On returning to the UK I was determined to use more quinoa in my cooking and this easy flatbread recipe is one of my favourites.

Method

1. Put the cooked quinoa to a food processor and pulse briefly.

2. Add the flours and pulse and then add the butter and pulse again to mix until you have a rubble like appearance.

3. Using the pulse button, add enough water until the mixture gathers into a soft dough (you may not need it all).

4. Remove from the processor and kneed for a minute to ensure that all of the ingredients are combined evenly in the dough. Cover with cling film and leave to rest for 10 minutes.

5. Divide the dough equally into 6 and roll each piece out into a thin circle. Lightly oil your skillet (or flat bottomed frying pan will work) and place over a medium heat.

6. Cook the first flatbread like a pancake until lightly browned before turning and cooking the other side.

7. Continue to cook the remaining flatbreads adding a little oil to the skillet each time as required.

8. Serve the flatbreads warm. A great accompaniment to salad or used to make a light sandwich.

Ingredients
Makes 6-8

- 50g quinoa, cooked and allowed to cool for 5 minutes
- 100g plain flour
- 100g whole wheat flour
- 60g butter (cut into small pieces)
- pinch of salt
- 125ml water
- olive oil for skillet

Tasty tips
For more colourful breads try using a mixture of red or black quinoa.

Pease Pudding

Ingredients

1 packet of toor dhal

Water to soak

800ml water or stock

1 onion, diced

4 rashers of smoked bacon, chopped

2 cloves garlic crushed

sprigs of fresh rosemary and thyme

3 bay leaves

Pease Pudding is a real north east favourite – it just wouldn't be a cookbook from Gateshead without it!

Method

1. Put the toor dhal into a large bowl and cover well with cold water. Soak overnight then drain and rinse thoroughly in a sieve.

2. Preheat oven to 180°C/gas mark 4.

3. Fry the onion, garlic and bacon in a little oil until golden and put into a large oven proof dish. Add the drained peas, rosemary and thyme and cover with 800ml of water or stock. Season with pepper only.

4. Cover with a lid or tin foil and bake for 1½ - 2 hours, stirring once or twice, until the lentils are tender and are the consistency of thick mushy peas, add extra water if the mixture gets a little dry. When tender add a large knob of butter and beat briskly with a wooden spoon to create a smoother texture then season to taste before serving.

5. Refrigerate the leftovers, they can be served hot or cold.

6. For cold pease pudding, simply cut off a slice and serve with meats or pâté.

Tasty tips

For hot pease pudding, cut off a slice and fry in butter until lightly golden on both sides

Index